Southern Living

Bookshelves & Cabinets

Oxmoor House®

Southern Living® Bookshelves and Cabinets was adapted from a book by the same title published by Sunset Books.

Consulting Editors: Don Vandervort, Jon Arno, Jane Horn
Editorial coordinator: Vicki Weathers

Senior Editors: Jim McRae, Pierre Home-Douglas
Art Director: Jean-Pierre Bourgeois
Writer: Stacey Berman
Researcher: Adam van Sertima
Picture Editor: Jennifer Meltzer

Special contributors:
  Gilles Beauchemin, Eric Beaulieu, Michel Blais,
  Linda Cardella Cournoyer, Jean-Guy Doiron,
  Lorraine Doré, Martin Francoeur, Michel Giguère,
  Sara Grynspan, Dominique Gagné, La Bande Créative,
  Robert Labelle, Anne-Marie Lemay, Jacques Perrault,
  Mathieu Raymond-Beaubien, Odette Sévigny,
  Jean Sirois, Judy Yelon

Cover: Design by Vasken Guiragossian.
Photography by Jean Allsopp.

Our appreciation to the staff of *Southern Living* magazine for their contributions to this book.

Acknowledgments
Thanks to the following:
American Hardboard Association, Palapine, IL
American Lumber Standards Committee, Germantown, MD
APA-The Engineered Wood Association, Tacoma, WA
Black & Decker Canada Inc., Mississauga, Ont.
Black & Decker Inc., Towson, MD
Borden Packaging and Industrial Products, Columbus, OH
Canadian Wood Council, Ottawa, Ont.
Delta International Machinery/Porter-Cable, Guelph, Ont.
Dewalt Industrial Tool Co., Hampstead, MD
Franklin International, Columbus, OH
Freud Inc., Mississauga, Ont.
Giles Miller-Mead, Brome, Que.
Mario Grosleau, Montreal, Que.
Hardwood Plywood & Veneer Association, Reston, VA
Hitachi Power Tools Ltd., Norcross/Atlanta, GA
Jet Equipment and Tools, Auburn, WA
Makita Canada Inc., Whitby, Ont.
Maze Nails, Peru, IL
McFeely's, Lynchburg, VA
Milwaukee Electric Tool Corp., Brookfield, WI
National Hardwood Lumber Assn., Memphis, TN
National Particleboard Association, Gaithersburg, MD
National Retail Hardware Association/*Do-It-Yourself Retailing Magazine*, Indianapolis, IN
Northwestern Steel and Wire, Sterling, IL
Marty Obando, Elizabeth City, NC
Occupational Safety and Health Association, Washington, DC
Pratt & Lambert/United Solvents of America, Sumter, SC
Ryobi North America Inc., Anderson, SC
Sears/Craftsman, Hoffman Estates, IL
Sherwin Williams Co., Cleveland, OH
Skil Canada, Markham, Ont.
United States Public Health Department, Washington, DC
Adam van Sertima, Montreal, Que.
Western Wood Products Association, Portland, OR

First printing January 1999
Copyright © 1999 by Oxmoor House, Inc.
Book Division of Southern Progress Corporation
P.O. Box 2463, Birmingham, Alabama 35201

Southern Living® is a federally registered trademark of Southern Living, Inc.

ISBN 0-376-09056-1
Library of Congress Catalog Card Number: 98-87041
Printed in the United States

Picture Credits
Photos courtesy of the following:
p. 4 Norman McGrath
p. 5 *(all)* Southern Living, Inc.
p. 6 *(both)* Crandall & Crandall
p. 7 *(upper)* Norman McGrath
    (lower) Crandall & Crandall
p. 8 *(upper)* Crandall & Crandall
    (lower) Emily Minton
p. 9 Jean Allsopp
p. 10 *(upper)* Emily Minton
    (lower) Jean Allsopp
p. 11 Robert Chartier
p. 12 *(all)* Crandall & Crandall
p. 13 Cheryl Dalton
p. 14 *(both)* Crandall & Crandall
p. 15 *(both)* Crandall & Crandall
p. 16 Robert Chartier

CONTENTS

BOOKSHELVES AND CABINETS

Bookshelves and cabinets add a warmth and coziness to any home, allowing you to display your favorite books, and also some of the family heirlooms, fine china, and knickknacks that lend a personal character to where you live.

But don't overlook their practical function too. These pieces of furniture can help you organize and store a myriad of items that might otherwise clutter up your home.

In this book, you'll learn how to build your own bookshelves and cabinets, from choosing stock and making cuts to assembling the units and adding the appropriate finish. The book concludes with a range of plans that will suit just about any home, from a simple TV and VCR stand to an elegant corner cabinet.

But first, let's take a look at what bookshelves and cabinets can offer you.

The graceful curve of the bay window in this home is mirrored in the custom-made bookcase beneath it.

The matching bookshelves in the living room shown at right create a symmetry that is perfectly in keeping with the formal style of the room. Archways and pilasters embellish the simple design of the bookshelves with classical motifs.

Cased openings in the room shown above give the depth needed for the bookshelves that frame them on three sides. Base cabinets provide concealed storage.

The open concept of this living room is accentuated by the wall-sized bookshelves. The fan-shaped windows above the unit provide plenty of light for reading and writing.

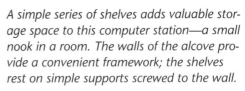

A simple series of shelves adds valuable storage space to this computer station—a small nook in a room. The walls of the alcove provide a convenient framework; the shelves rest on simple supports screwed to the wall.

Corners of a room are often lost space. Here, a triangular cabinet makes the most of the available room, while doubling as camouflage for a portion of the stainless-steel chimney.

One of the problems with high bookshelves and cabinets is that the upper shelves are often difficult to access. Here, a track secured near the top of the unit provides a support for a wooden ladder that can be shifted easily to where it is needed.

The bookshelf in this den is basically a simple structure, but topped off with crown molding it has a more formal look that fits in well with the coffered ceiling and paneled walls that surround it.

The bookshelf shown above performs double duty as a bookcase and room divider. Built twice the depth of a normal bookcase, it can be accessed from both sides of the unit.

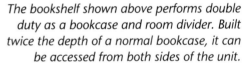

This bookcase offers no hint that it's also a doorway to a home office. To support its weight, the unit was mounted with extra heavy-duty hinges hidden by a 3-inch lip on the outside frame.
Designer: Ginger Kelly.

Built-in bookshelves that adjust in height can accommodate a changing display of family photographs and collectibles, as well as favorite books. The nook for the window seat provides natural light and a cozy retreat for reading.
Interior designer: Kimberly Bean.

A freestanding bookcase needn't always hug the wall. In this formal living room, a low, shallow bookcase with drawers fits perfectly behind the exposed back of a sofa and becomes a focal point in the room. Designer: Landy Gardner.

This unit provides plenty of room for storing books, video-cassettes, electronic equipment, and games, along with an entertainment area that puts the television front and center.

An armoire can add a touch of old-world charm to any room. Glass doors allow for easy display while keeping dust away from books.

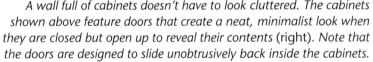

A wall full of cabinets doesn't have to look cluttered. The cabinets shown above feature doors that create a neat, minimalist look when they are closed but open up to reveal their contents (right). Note that the doors are designed to slide unobtrusively back inside the cabinets.

This cabinet boasts an ingenious space-saving device—the unit holding the television raises and lowers as needed. With the TV retracted back inside the cabinet, the surface of the unit can be used for display. Side drawers contribute to the overall storage potential.

An extension of the cooking island provides handy storage space for cookbooks, as well as a wine rack. As the shelves face away from the cooktop, contents are shielded from spills and spatters.
Architects: Frank McAlpine and Bill Ingram. Interior designer: Janice Howerton.

Space is often at a premium in many kitchens. The designers of the unit shown at left maximized its storage space by installing adjustable shelves and doors that feature their own sets of shelving.

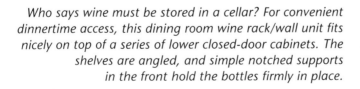

Who says wine must be stored in a cellar? For convenient dinnertime access, this dining room wine rack/wall unit fits nicely on top of a series of lower closed-door cabinets. The shelves are angled, and simple notched supports in the front hold the bottles firmly in place.

A series of glass-doored cabinets fits snugly between ceiling-high vertical columns, perfectly complementing the light, spacious feel of this living room.

The upper and lower cabinets in the bedroom at left offer plenty of storage possibilities, along with a desk/workstation created by leaving space between two cabinets. Open glass display shelves in the upper cabinet add a homey feel to the room.

BUILDING MATERIALS

The final appearance of your bookshelf or cabinet depends as much on the materials you use as the workmanship that goes into it. As a rule of thumb, it's best to choose the highest-quality materials your budget allows. This doesn't necessarily mean opting for solid wood over plywood and manufactured panels *(page 22)*, for example, as the latter can often provide both beauty and structural integrity at a lower cost.

As well as wood, this chapter will feature the hardware that goes into a typical project. From the fasteners that hold the unit together, shown on pages 24 and 25, to the hinges necessary for doors *(page 27)* and brackets for shelving *(page 29)*, the information provided will help you build a solid piece. And once it's built, choosing the right finish will give it a professional look. Turn to page 31 for a list of finishing products.

Bookshelves and cabinets can be built from materials ranging from solid wood to manufactured panels. To help you decide on the material that's best for your project, see the information beginning on the opposite page.

LUMBER FOR YOUR NEEDS

Beautiful, long-lasting wooden cabinets and book-cases could not be possible without good lumber. To find the right boards for your project, it's best that you go to the lumberyard with some basic understanding of wood: Size, species, and grade must be taken into account. Make sure you understand these basic terms, and do your homework first. Determine the kind of wood you want to buy, then calculate the exact size of every piece required for your project—adding some for the inevitable wastage. The more careful and complete your planning, the easier it will be to find and buy exactly what you need. If you'd prefer to use manufactured boards, see page 22.

Softwood and hardwood: Solid lumber is divided into softwoods, from conifers, and hardwoods, from deciduous trees. As their name implies, hardwoods are usually harder. But some softwoods, such as Douglas-fir and southern pine, are actually harder than hardwoods such as poplar, aspen, or lauan. As a rule, softwoods are less expensive, easier to work with, and more readily available. However, the more durable hardwoods have greater richness and diversity of color, grain, and texture. Turn to page 20 for more on the characteristics and uses of a variety of softwoods and hardwoods.

HOW LUMBER IS SOLD

Before you head out to the lumberyard to buy your stock, you should know about board measure, nominal size, and moisture content of wood.

Board measure: Softwoods are sold either by the lineal foot or by the board foot; hardwoods are sold by the lineal foot, by the board foot, or for very dense or expensive types, by the pound. The lineal foot, commonly used for small orders, considers only the piece's length. For example, you might ask for seven 1x10s, each 6 feet long, or 42 lineal feet of 1x10.

The board foot—the equivalent of a board 1 inch thick and 1 foot long and wide—is the most common unit for volume orders. To compute board feet, use this formula: (thickness in inches) x (width in inches $\geqslant$ 12) x (length in feet). For example, a 1x12 board 8 feet long would be computed: $1" \times 12" \geqslant 12 \times 8' = 8$ board feet.

Nominal and surfaced (actual) sizes: A common mistake is assuming that a 2x4 board is actually 2 inches thick and 4 inches wide. These numbers are actually the lumber's nominal size—its size when sliced from the log. As the chart at right shows, the piece's size is reduced when dried and surfaced (planed). Available lengths range from 6 to 20 feet, in increments of 2 feet. Most softwood lumber is surfaced on four sides (designated S4S), but some species are also sold rough, or unsurfaced, remaining close to the nominal dimensions.

Buying hardwoods can be tricky, because they come in random widths and lengths, seemingly odd thicknesses, and are often rough-edged. For boards 1 inch or more thick, you may see the term four quarter or 4/4. This is a hardwood's nominal thickness—so a 4/4 board is about 1 inch thick, a 5/4 board about 1¼ inches thick, and so on. Hardwoods are normally surfaced thicker than softwoods; see the chart below. Standard lengths range from 4 to 16 feet, in increments of one foot.

The designations S1S, S2S, S3S, and S4S mean surfaced one side, two sides, etc. Hardwoods are often sold S2S, with both faces planed. S1E indicates that the board has been surfaced on one edge; S2E means both edges. Combined, the wood designations can be something like S2S1E (surfaced two sides and one edge). Unless you have a planer, buy S2S or ask the yard to mill the boards to the exact thickness.

Moisture content (MC): When wood is sawn, it's still "green" (unseasoned). The best lumber is then dried, either by air or kiln. Kiln-drying, the more expensive process, reduces the moisture content to any desired level. Use "dry" lumber for your bookshelves, cabinets, and other furniture. Hardwoods are mostly kiln-dried (KD) to about 6-8%, but not surfaced until they acclimate to about 10-12%; softwoods come either air- or kiln-dried, or green. Choose wood stamped "MC 15," which indicates that the moisture content when the wood was surfaced did not exceed 15%, although "S-DRY" or "KD," with a maximum MC of 19%, is usually stable enough. Green wood will most likely split, warp, or shrink unless dried properly—it isn't recommended for shelves or cabinets.

STANDARD DIMENSIONS OF SOFTWOODS		STANDARD THICKNESSES OF HARDWOODS	
Nominal size	Surfaced dry (actual) size	Rough	Surfaced 2 Sides
1x2	¾"x1½"	⅜"	3/16"
1x3	¾"x2½"	½"	5/16"
1x4	¾"x3½"	⅝"	7/16"
1x6	¾"x5½"	¾"	9/16"
1x8	¾"x7¼"	1"	13/16" or ¾"
1x10	¾"x9¼"	1¼"	1 1/16"
1x12	¾"x11¼"	1½"	1 5/16"
2x2	1½"x1½"	1¾"	1½"
2x4	1½"x3½"	2"	1¾"
2x6	1½"x5½"	2½"	2¼"
2x8	1½"x7¼"	3"	2¾"

MAKING THE GRADE

At the mill, lumber of the same species and size is sorted into grades, then identified with a grade stamp (mainly used on softwoods) or inventoried by species or grade. Different lumberyards may use different grade names; when in doubt, ask for help. Grade distinctions are based on defects. You can save money by choosing the lowest acceptable grade that you can live with.

Softwood grades: The two basic categories are dimension lumber and appearance boards—use the latter for this book's projects. The most common grading system, from the Western Wood Products Association, has four main board categories, each with different grades. Use Select and Finish grades when appearance counts. Common grades tend to look knotty. Alternate board grades (Construction, Standard, Utility, Select Merchantable, and Economy) should be avoided unless intended for a hidden part of the project or painted. Use high-grade dimension lumber for extra strength or thickness. See the softwood grading chart at right for more information.

Select grades are B&BTR (best appearance; often clear), C-Select (very good appearance; fine finish), and D-Select (good appearance; when finish isn't as vital). **Finish** grades include Superior (the highest grade, with completely clear boards), Prime (very good appearance), and E (with defects that can be cut off). **Common** grades range from 1 to 5. For making attractive bookshelves and cabinets, use 2&Better Common (a combination of 1 and 2 Common; boards with a good, knotty appearance), and 3 Common; avoid 4 and 5 Common.

To complicate the issue further, certain lumber species have their own grading systems. For instance, the Idaho white pine (IWP) grades are Supreme,

SOME SOFTWOOD GRADES	
Grade	Characteristics
Select B&BTR (Supreme)	Highest quality, almost completely clear (minor defects). Use with clear finishes. May not be readily available; can be costly.
C Select (Choice)	High quality, with slight defects and blemishes.
D Select (Quality)	Good quality wood, with more pronounced defects and blemishes.
Superior Finish	The highest quality of all finish grade lumber; with minor defects and blemishes.
Prime Finish	High quality; a few defects and blemishes.
No. 1 Common (Colonial)	Limited availability; limited size range; can have small knots; good for producing knotty look.
No. 2 Common (Sterling)	Larger, more coarse defects and blemishes; often used to produce knotty appearance.

SOME HARDWOOD LUMBER GRADES				
Grade	FAS	Select	No. 1 Common	Nos. 2A & 2B Common
Allowable board length	8'-16'	6'-16'	4'-16'	4'-16'
Allowable board width	6" or wider	4" or wider	3" or wider	3" or wider
Minimal % of clear face cuttings	83 1/3%	83 1/3%	66 2/3%	50%
Minimum size of clear cuttings	3"x7'; 4"x5'	3"x7'; 4"x5'	3"x3'; 4"x2'	3"x2'
Formula for number of cuts	Surface Measure (SM)÷4	SM÷4	SM+1÷3	SM÷2
Maximum clear cuttings	4	4	5	7

Choice, Quality, Colonial, Sterling, Standard, Utility, and Industrial.

For a perfect finish, use defect-free boards. Buy a lower grade if the wood won't be visible, or if you plan to paint. Be careful about using less-expensive Number 2 and 3 Common boards. Use lower grades with one defect-free face when one side will show.

Hardwood grades: As with softwood, the number of defects in a given length and width of hardwood determines the grade. The grades used by the National Hardwood Lumber Association include: Firsts, Seconds, Selects, No. 1 Common, No. 2A Common, No. 3A Common, and No. 3B Common. Select and Better is a combination grade used at most mills and the one favored by cabinetmakers. It will have some Firsts and Seconds, making it good for producing "clear" furniture; defects can usually be cut out and still yield usable pieces. In that regard, it offers the best price value. If your project calls for small pieces, No. 1 Common is an economical choice.

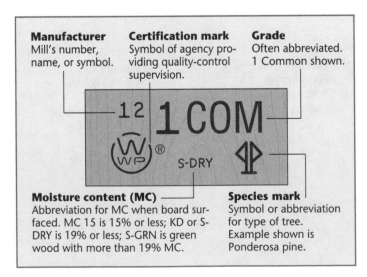

Manufacturer
Mill's number, name, or symbol.

Certification mark
Symbol of agency providing quality-control supervision.

Grade
Often abbreviated. 1 Common shown.

Moisture content (MC)
Abbreviation for MC when board surfaced. MC 15 is 15% or less; KD or S-DRY is 19% or less; S-GRN is green wood with more than 19% MC.

Species mark
Symbol or abbreviation for type of tree. Example shown is Ponderosa pine.

Reading a grade stamp
The above marking is an example of a grade stamp used by the Western Wood Products Association. If a stamp is applied to appearance grades of lumber, it will be on the back or edge.

OTHER CHARACTERISTICS OF LUMBER

Even within the same grade of lumber, individual pieces may differ. When possible, sort through the stacks at the lumberyard yourself; most yards will allow this providing you repile the stacks when you're done.

Vertical and flat grain: Depending on how the board is cut from the log, there will be either parallel grain lines running the length of the piece (vertical grain) or a marbled appearance (flat grain), as shown in the illustration below. Vertical grain results from quarter-sawing—a cut nearly perpendicular to the annual growth rings. It's stronger and less likely to warp or shrink noticeably. Flat grain arises when pieces are flat-sawn, or cut tangential to the growth rings. Flat sawing can sometimes produce attractive figures, or patterns, from the combination of knots, crotches, pores, and growth rings that are present in any given tree.

Heartwood and sapwood: The inactive wood nearest the center of a living tree is called heartwood. Sapwood, next to the bark, contains the growth cells. The main differences are color and density; heartwood is usually darker, denser, and more decay-resistant than sapwood.

Defects: Lumber may contain defects from either weathering or milling; many of these are shown in the chart at right. Examine each board closely before buying it. To test for warping, lift each piece by one end and sight down the face and edges. Pieces with long, gentle bends can sometimes be machined flat, but unless you can work around the defect, it's best to reject the board. Other defects include checks, (cracks in the surface or ends of the board), shakes (separations along annual growth rings), and honeycombing (hollows between annual rings). Also look for general problems such as rotting, staining, insect holes, and pitch pockets (sap reservoirs below the surface). Try to avoid the "bull's-eye pieces" milled from the center of the log; they tend to crack and warp more easily than other pieces.

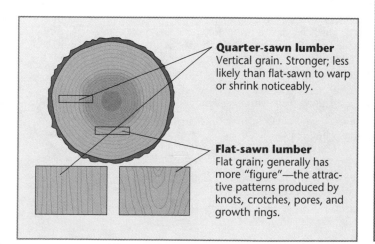

Quarter-sawn lumber
Vertical grain. Stronger; less likely than flat-sawn to warp or shrink noticeably.

Flat-sawn lumber
Flat grain; generally has more "figure"—the attractive patterns produced by knots, crotches, pores, and growth rings.

COMMON LUMBER DEFECTS

Defect	Description	What to do
Crook	Warp along the edge line; also known as crown.	Straighten the edge on a jointer.
Bow	Warp on the face of a board from end to end.	Cut the piece into shorter, unbowed pieces, or remove the bow by face-jointing on a jointer.
Cup	Hollow across the face of a board.	Dry the piece until both faces have equal moisture content, or rip the piece into narrower, usable pieces.
Twist	Multiple bends in a board.	Cut and use in shorter lengths, or face-joint to remove the twist.
Knot or knothole	A tight knot is not usually a problem; a loose or dead knot, surrounded by a dark ring, may fall out later, or may already have left a hole.	Cut off the part with a knot or knothole; remove any loose knots before machining the lumber. Sound knots may be kept if a knotty look is desired.
Check	Cracks along the grain not passing through the entire thickness of the wood.	Cut off or fill (page 80) the checked portion.
Split	Crack going all the way through the piece of wood, commonly at the ends.	Cut off the split part of the board.
Shake	Separation of grain between the growth rings, often extending along the board's face, and sometimes below its surface.	Cut off the shake.
Wane	Missing wood or untrimmed bark along the edge or corner of the piece.	Edge-joint or cut off the affected part.

A GUIDE TO WOOD SPECIES

The weekend woodworker who buys the occasional plank of pine or maple at a small local lumberyard is often not aware of the extraordinary diversity of wood that is available. More than 900 species exist in the United States alone, and thousands more worldwide. That range is reflected in the wide variety of colors and grain patterns available, from the vivid reds of padauk to the warm, brown hues of walnut. Even among the same species there is considerable variation. Black cherry, for example, can vary from a palish brown to a rich red, and the figure of the wood can look different depending on whether the board was flat-sawn or quarter-sawn *(page 19)*.

Since the wood you choose can be as important as the actual design of a piece of furniture, it's worth taking the time to consider what building materials you will use for your project. The charts on these two pages present a range of softwoods and hardwoods available to the woodworker. The hardwoods are divided into two groups: domestic and exotic. The latter group contain some of the most cherished woods for cabinetmakers, such as teak and bocote. These woods tend to be much more expensive than their domestic counterparts, and they are often difficult to work with because of their hardness. Before you build a cabinet or bookcase from them, experiment first with a smaller piece of furniture to gain some practice. Also, you can sometimes find inexpensive alternatives to more costly woods. Lauan, for example, is commonly used as an economical substitute for mahogany.

If you have trouble locating any of the woods listed in the following charts at your lumberyard, check out mail-order wood specialty companies, which advertise in woodworking magazines.

COMMON SOFTWOODS	
Species	**Characteristics**
Cedar, Alaska yellow	Pale yellow; heavy, strong, more stable than other cedars. Very resistant to decay and splintering. Easily worked; has slightly unpleasant odor when cut. Limited availability; expensive.
Cedar, aromatic	Noted for ivory sapwood and dark red heartwood. Also known as eastern red cedar; used in cedar chests and as closet lining since it discourages insects. Defect-prone but easily worked.
Cedar, western red	Handsome grain, wide color variation (ivory to pink, russet, red), decay-resistant. Soft and weak, but versatile. Works easily; takes glue, finishes well. Stable when dry. Widely available.
Bald cypress	Typically straight-grain; yellow to amber tones. Hard, strong, moderately heavy; oily texture; good decay resistance. Machines easily, shrinks little. Holds nails reasonably well. Often used in high-moisture areas (saunas, greenhouses) as well as for millwork. Good for water containers and utensils; doesn't impart taste, odor, or color. Available largely in its native Southeast.
Douglas-fir/western larch	Straight-grain, orange-colored; pronounced stripes. Resinous; exceptionally strong and stiff. Often sold together, fir being predominant. Quarter-sawn boards produce beautiful vertical grain suitable for cabinets and millwork; also highly valued for structural uses. Both work fairly well with sharp tools; avoid using heavily pigmented stains due to differences in grain density.
Hemlock, eastern/balsam fir	Similar to western types. Coarse texture, strong (balsam fir less so), and resin-free.
Hemlock, western/true firs	Cream-colored, bland woods generally sold together as "Hem-fir" (the firs include several western species). Light, moderately strong; shrinkage and warping can be serious problem unless wood is bone-dry. Easily worked. Accepts glue and paint moderately well.
Pine, eastern white/western (Idaho white, sugar, lodgepole, Ponderosa)	Very white to russet. Soft and relatively weak; ideal for shaping. Smooth and uniform; knots and pitch pockets common. Little checking or warping. Hold fasteners moderately well with little splitting. Eastern white, Idaho white (western white), and sugar known for satiny surface and workability. Lodgepole is stable, straight-grain wood found in narrow widths. Ponderosa ("knotty pine") is versatile and popular.
Pine, southern yellow (pitch, shortleaf, longleaf, loblolly)	White to yellowish woods; hard, strong, and moderately heavy. Generally coarse in texture and full of resin. Work and finish relatively well, with excellent nail-holding ability.
Redwood	Red to russet and pink heartwood; creamy white sapwood. Heartwood highly resistant to decay and insects. Lightweight and fine-textured. Quite soft; scratches, splinters, and dents easily. Produces wide, often clear, resin-free lumber. Works easily; finishes beautifully. Holds fasteners only moderately well; prone to splitting. Becoming rare. Expensive outside the West.
Spruce, eastern	Nondescript, whitish wood; uniform in grain. Relatively soft; strong for its weight; stable. Works easily, resists splitting; takes paint and fasteners well.
Spruce, Sitka	Creamy to pinkish brown; wide, clear lumber with straight grain. Very strong for its weight. Works easily; planes to silky sheen. Resists splintering.

HARDWOODS

Domestic species	Characteristics
Alder, red	Pinkish brown with little figure. Easy to work. Often substituted for birch, but less hard and strong. Poor durability in exterior applications. Inexpensive.
Ash, white	Creamy to grayish brown; tough, strong and very shock-resistant, open-grain wood, but with poor durability. Versatile; works easily; accepts finishes well. Heartwood commonly has different markings of different colors, which are known by the names olive ash or calico ash. Moderately priced.
Basswood	Nondescript, creamy white to russet "woodcarver's wood." Lightweight, soft, uniform grain and very fine-textured. Very good workability; can slightly blunt saw blades. Accepts glue and paint well; stable. Moderately priced.
Beech	Tan to reddish in color; conspicuous rays and tiny pores. Even, fine texture. Heavy and hard; prone to checking and warping. Works fairly well, but may burn when crosscut or drilled. Accepts finishes well. Moderately priced.
Birch, yellow	Light reddish brown with pleasing grain. Hard, heavy, and strong. Versatile; machines easily and accepts finishes well. Moderately priced.
Cherry, black	Uniform, reddish brown color with attractive figure. Fine grain and smooth texture. Extremely stable, strong, and hard, but not heavy. Works well; takes satiny finish. Darkens with age. Most contain gum deposits throughout, which can show on veneers. Moderately priced.
Hickory/pecan	White to reddish brown; fairly uniform grain, but can be wavy or irregular. Strong, hard, flexible woods; often sold together. Must be seasoned carefully. Very tough and elastic; more difficult to work, but has good bending properties. Moderately priced.
Maple, hard	White to reddish tan; great variety of grain, including curly, wavy, and bird's-eye. Heavy, hard, but nondurable. Difficult to work, can blunt cutting edges, but accepts finishes well; resistant to abuse and abrasion. Moderately priced.
Oak, red	Very popular pinkish wood; most common oak in North America. Fairly straight-grained with large pores; coarse texture. Heavy, hard, and moderately durable. Machines well, but can blunt cutting tools. Finishes well, but fill open pores before finishing or painting. Moderately priced.
Oak, white	Yellowish brown in color with distinctive quarter-sawn rays and closed pores. Dense, strong, and very durable. Straight grain with moderately coarse texture. Machines and finishes well; good bending properties. Moderately expensive.
Poplar, yellow	Yellowish brown to olive green heartwood; bland, uniform grain. Fine, even texture. Light and moderately soft. Works easily; can slightly dull cutting tools. Accepts finishes well; no grain shows through paint. Inexpensive.
Walnut, black	Chocolate brown wood; handsome figure. Mostly straight grain with medium-coarse texture. Durable and strong, with good shock resistance. Works well, takes high polish; very stable. Contains the chemical juglone, thought to cause dermatitis in some woodworkers. Expensive.

Exotic species	Characteristics
Bocote	Brown to black wood with yellow lines; sometimes called Mexican rosewood. Straight to wavy grain. Heavy, hard, and oily. Expensive.
Koa	Golden brown Hawaiian wood with some fiddleback figure. Hard, strong, difficult to work, but finishes to lustrous sheen. Very rare, hard to find. Expensive.
Lauan	Tan to reddish "Philippine mahogany"; large pores and much ribbon grain. Various lauans differ in color, texture, and density. Coarser, stringier, and less stable than true mahoganies; doesn't machine as well. Moderately priced.
Mahogany (African, and Central and South American)	Golden to reddish brown wood with variable grain; much figure. Moderately soft; very strong and durable; exceptionally stable. Works very well. Large, clear pieces available. Moderately expensive.
Padauk	Strong and vivid red in color; uniform, coarse texture; good for contrast. Hard heavy wood; machines well. Expensive.
Purpleheart	Mildly striped wood (properly called amaranth) from American tropics; turns royal purple after cutting. Straight grain with a moderate to coarse texture. Durable, hard, and stringy; difficult to work. Accepts finishes well. Moderately expensive.
Satinwood, Ceylon	Yellow to gold, with beautiful figure. Fine, even texture. Used for centuries in fine woodworking and cabinetmaking. Difficult to work; accepts finishes well when filled. Expensive.
Teak	Golden brown Southeast Asian wood; some similarities to walnut. Oily; very strong, stable, durable outdoors. Straight to wavy grain. May be hard on saw blades, and may cause skin rash and/or respiratory problems. Hard to glue. Expensive.

SHEET PRODUCTS

Although solid lumber is the preferred choice for high-quality, beautifully crafted bookshelves and cabinets, manufactured wood panels such as plywood, hardboard, and particleboard are very attractive and practical alternatives. For one, these are available in many thicknesses and sizes, with or without decorative grooves, patterns, and veneers. They also are dimensionally stable, come in large sheets, and generally cost less than solid lumber.

Plywood, the most familiar of the sheet products, is used extensively for furniture and doors. Use standard hardboard for cabinet backs. Perforated hardboard, known by its tradename, Peg-Board, is often combined with hooks for hanging storage. Particleboard is used for shelving, as core stock for pieces to be laminated or veneered, or in other hidden applications.

Plywood: Plywood is made from thin wood veneers peeled from the log then glued together. The veneer grain runs perpendicular to the layers just above and below, so plywood is strong in all directions. Standard sheet size is 4 feet by 8 feet; 10-foot-long sheets can be ordered. Like solid lumber, plywoods are divided into softwood and hardwood types, according to the face and back veneers only.

Softwood plywood: Made from up to 70 different species of wood, the most common softwood plywoods are Douglas-fir and southern yellow pine. Species are grouped according to stiffness and strength; Group 1 is the strongest and Group 5 the weakest. Panels are also rated by grade, based on the face and back appearances, (see the chart on the next page for more information). The N grade has a perfect, natural finish, but it has to be special-ordered; even so, it's rarely available. Generally, presanded A and B grades are the best choices where wood will be visible; lower grades are unsuitable for a fine finish. Plywood is available in many face/back grade combinations, though your lumberyard may stock only a few. If both sides of the material will be exposed, choose A/B panels. A/C or A/D panels are economical choices when only one side will be visible. These and other characteristics are shown on the stamp imprinted on the back or edge of each panel (*below*). Always look for the face and back grades and exposure rating.

Standard softwood plywood is commonly available from 1/4 to 3/4 inch thick, in 1/8-inch increments.

Hardwood plywood: Though more expensive than softwood, this is an economical and stable alternative to solid hardwood. It's identified by the veneer used on the face side of the panel. Popular domestic faces include ash, birch, black walnut, cherry, maple, and oak. A number of imported woods are also available. Standard panel size is 4 feet by 8 feet; common thicknesses are 1/8 inch, 1/4 inch, 3/8 inch, 1/2 inch, and 3/4 inch.

Hardwood plywood is graded differently than the softwood type. See the chart on the next page. Face grades range from AA, used for the highest-quality projects, to E. With its excellent appearance, A is a good choice for furniture. For hidden areas, or where the natural appearance is desired, use B (less uniform than A), or the C, D, and E grouping (more color variation and repairs). Back grades are rated from 1 to 4, with 1 being the most sound. A term such as A2 indicates that the face is grade A and the back is grade 2; face and back veneers are commonly the same species. On most better-quality panels, look for the grade stamp on the edge of the panel; back-stamps are avoided because they mar the surface.

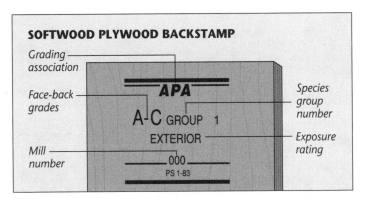

SOFTWOOD PLYWOOD BACKSTAMP

Grading association

Face-back grades

Mill number

APA

A-C GROUP 1

EXTERIOR

000
PS 1-83

Species group number

Exposure rating

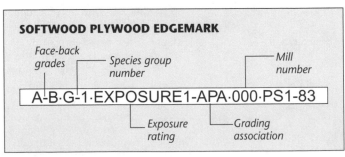

SOFTWOOD PLYWOOD EDGEMARK

Face-back grades

Species group number

Mill number

A·B·G·1·EXPOSURE1·APA·000·PS1-83

Exposure rating

Grading association

One of the most popular face species for hardwood plywoods is birch; it's durable and attractive, machines cleanly, and is one of the lowest-priced hardwood plywoods. You can increase your savings by choosing "shop" birch plywood if you can work around the slight defects found on those panels.

Some grades of plywood may have voids in the inner veneers; these show up on exposed edges. Putty the edges, cover them with veneer or molding, or buy lumber-core sheets; made of face veneers glued to a solid core, this plywood has easily worked edges and holds fasteners much better than veneer-core plywood.

If you plan to clear-finish the edges or are looking for extra strength in thin sheets, try to obtain some Baltic (which may also be known as Russian or Finnish) birch panels made up of many very thin, solid veneers. They come in sheets that measure 5 by 5 or 8 by 4 feet (the grain runs across the width).

Hardboard: Hardboard is made by reducing waste wood chips to fibers, then bonding these together under pressure with adhesives. Harder, denser, and cheaper than plywood, hardboard is commonly produced in 4- by 8-foot sheets. It can be smooth on both sides or have a meshlike texture on the back. There are two main types: standard hardboard is easily painted, while the tempered type, designed for strength and moisture resistance, is hard to paint. Hardboard is available in 1/8- and 1/4-inch thicknesses. Though easy to cut and shape, it quickly dulls standard tools; use carbide-tipped blades and router bits. Always drill a pilot hole when fastening.

Similar but less dense, fiberboard is available in thicker sheets; a common type is medium-density fiberboard, or MDF. It has a smooth, even surface, and can replace solid wood; it machines well, leaving crisp edges that don't need to be covered up with edge-banding or molding. To screw into MDF, drill a pilot hole first.

Particleboard: Made from particles of waste wood that are bonded together, particleboard has a speckled appearance. Its advantages are a smooth surface and consistent flatness. Standard sheet size is 4 by 8 feet; common thicknesses range from 1/4 inch to 2 inches in 1/16-inch increments. Several types of particleboard, with different-size particles, are available under different names. The most common is a single-layer sheet with uniform density and particle size. When possible, choose the triple-layer type with a denser, smoother face and back.

Particleboard tends to sag; for shelves or any other horizontal surface, always support it at close intervals. You can cut and shape particleboard with standard tools, but equip power tools with carbide-tipped saw blades and router bits. Drill a pilot hole for fasteners. Avoid using water-base finishing products; the water soaks in, causing some of the particles to swell. Any visible edges are commonly covered by edge-banding or molding.

THE SOFTWOOD PLYWOOD GRADING SYSTEM	
Grade	**Characteristics**
N	Smooth surface "natural finish" veneer. Select, all heartwood or all sapwood. Free of open defects. Allows not more than 6 repairs, wood only, per 4x8 panel, made parallel to grain and well-matched for grain and color.
A	Smooth, paintable. Not more than 18 neatly made repairs, boat, sled, or router type, and parallel to grain permitted. May be used for natural finish in less demanding applications. Synthetic repairs permitted.
B	Solid surface. Shims, circular repair plugs, and tight knots to 1" across grain permitted, as are synthetic repairs and some minor splits.
C-Plugged	Improved C veneer with splits limited to 1/8" width and knotholes and borer holes limited to 1/4" x 1/2". Admits some broken grain. Synthetic repairs permitted.
C	Tight knots to 1 1/2". Knotholes to 1" across grain and some to 1 1/2" if total width of knots and knotholes is within specified limits. Synthetic or wood repairs. Discoloration and sanding defects that do not impair strength permitted. Limited splits allowed. Stitching permitted.
D	Knots and knotholes to 2 1/2" width across grain and 1/2" larger within specified limits. Limited splits are permitted. Stitching permitted. Limited to Exposure 1, or interior panels.

THE HARDWOOD PLYWOOD GRADING SYSTEM	
Grade	**Characteristics**
A grade (Premium)	Smooth face veneer with well-matched seams; made of specific hardwood, like walnut or mahogany. No grain or color contrasts.
B grade (Good)	Face veneer similar to premium, but not as well matched. No sharp color and grain contrasts.
Sound (2)	Face veneer smooth, but not matched for grain or color. Defects only on back veneer. Best when painted or stained.
Utility	Veneers have rough grain and may have knotholes up to 3/4", some discoloration, staining, and slight splits. Not matched for color and grain.
Back	May have larger defects than the Utility grade, but panel strength is not impaired. Not matched for color or grain.
Specialty (SP)	Made to order to meet specific requirements, like separate panels with matching grain patterns.

FASTENERS

No matter what type of bookshelf or cabinet you plan to make, you will have to join pieces of wood. And that means that you'll need to choose the appropriate fastener. Nailing is the quickest way to attach wood, but it offers a limited amount of holding power. When the project demands extra strength, a combination of screws and adhesives is usually preferred.

Bolts are stronger than either nails or screws. Most bolts are made from zinc-plated steel, but you can also buy the brass and stainless-steel types when appearance or corrosion resistance counts.

Knockdown (K-D) hardware is often used in factory-built furniture to join components that meet in simple butt joints. Two types of knockdown hardware are available. One type allows you to disassemble the components for storage or transport; the other joins pieces permanently.

When used correctly, a good adhesive creates a joint that is at least as strong as the wood itself. Adhesives vary according to strength, water resistance, ability to fill gaps, and setting time. For general work, most woodworkers rely on white or yellow glue.

NAILS AND SCREWS

The array of different screws available to the woodworker can be bewildering. The most commonly used screws for woods are shown below. Drywall screws are becoming increasingly popular with woodworkers. These versatile fasteners are a big improvement over traditional wood screws: They're sharper and better machined, and the Phillips heads won't strip as easily. Screws are sized by length (from 1/4 to 4 inches), and for thickness, by wire gauge number (0 to 24—about 1/16 to 3/8 inch). The higher the gauge number for a given length of screw, the greater its holding ability. To measure screw length see the illustration at right.

Nail lengths may be indicated by the term "penny" (abbreviated as d). This once referred to the cost of 100 hand-forged nails; 3-penny nails, for example, were 3 cents per hundred. The illustration on the following page shows the equivalents in inches of some nail sizes. For cabinetmaking, 1 inch, 1 1/4 inches, and 1 1/2 inches are the lengths most commonly used.

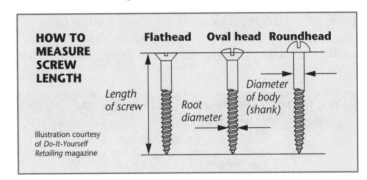

HOW TO MEASURE SCREW LENGTH

Flathead   Oval head   Roundhead

Length of screw

Root diameter

Diameter of body (shank)

Illustration courtesy of *Do-It-Yourself Retailing* magazine

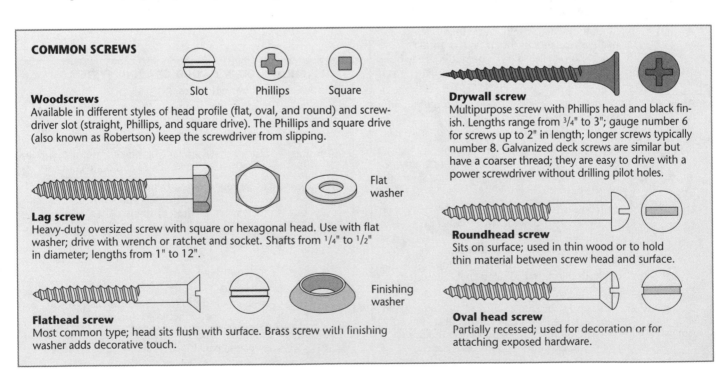

COMMON SCREWS

Slot   Phillips   Square

Woodscrews
Available in different styles of head profile (flat, oval, and round) and screwdriver slot (straight, Phillips, and square drive). The Phillips and square drive (also known as Robertson) keep the screwdriver from slipping.

Flat washer

Lag screw
Heavy-duty oversized screw with square or hexagonal head. Use with flat washer; drive with wrench or ratchet and socket. Shafts from 1/4 to 1/2" in diameter; lengths from 1" to 12".

Finishing washer

Flathead screw
Most common type; head sits flush with surface. Brass screw with finishing washer adds decorative touch.

Drywall screw
Multipurpose screw with Phillips head and black finish. Lengths range from 3/4" to 3"; gauge number 6 for screws up to 2" in length; longer screws typically number 8. Galvanized deck screws are similar but have a coarser thread; they are easy to drive with a power screwdriver without drilling pilot holes.

Roundhead screw
Sits on surface; used in thin wood or to hold thin material between screw head and surface.

Oval head screw
Partially recessed; used for decoration or for attaching exposed hardware.

KNOCKDOWN FITTINGS

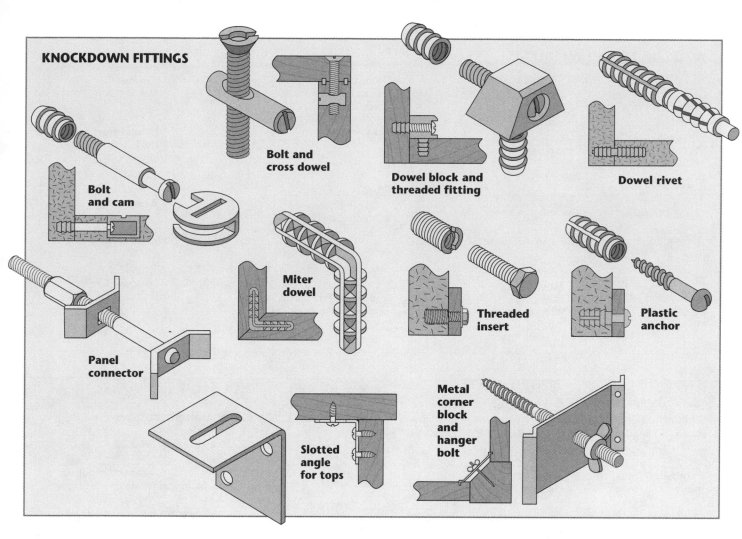

Bolt and cross dowel

Dowel block and threaded fitting

Dowel rivet

Bolt and cam

Miter dowel

Threaded insert

Plastic anchor

Panel connector

Slotted angle for tops

Metal corner block and hanger bolt

A NAIL FOR ALL REASONS

COMMON SIZES OF NAILS

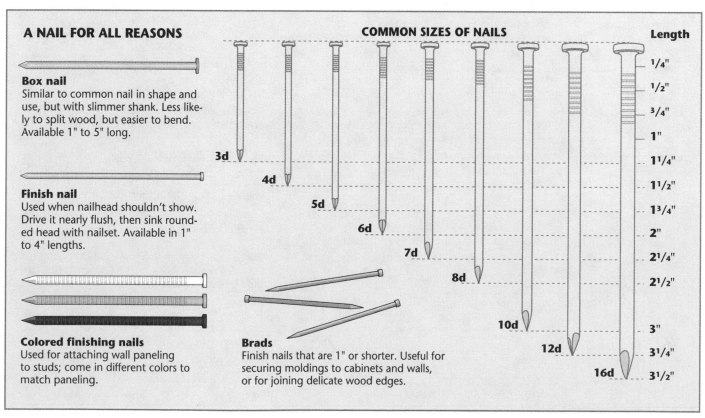

Box nail
Similar to common nail in shape and use, but with slimmer shank. Less likely to split wood, but easier to bend. Available 1" to 5" long.

Finish nail
Used when nailhead shouldn't show. Drive it nearly flush, then sink rounded head with nailset. Available in 1" to 4" lengths.

Colored finishing nails
Used for attaching wall paneling to studs; come in different colors to match paneling.

Brads
Finish nails that are 1" or shorter. Useful for securing moldings to cabinets and walls, or for joining delicate wood edges.

	Length
	1/4"
	1/2"
	3/4"
3d	1"
4d	1 1/4"
5d	1 1/2"
6d	1 3/4"
7d	2"
8d	2 1/4"
	2 1/2"
10d	3"
12d	3 1/4"
16d	3 1/2"

BOLTS, NUTS, AND WASHERS

Machine bolt
Hexagonal head driven with wrench.

Carriage bolt
Self-anchoring head digs into the wood as nut is tightened.

Stove bolt
Slotted for screwdrivers.

Flat washer
Most bolts need washers at each end. Self-anchoring bolts, such as carriage bolts, require only one washer, inside nut.

Wing nut
Quickly tightened or loosened by hand.

T-nut
Driven flush into bottom material, preventing it from rotating. Weaker than other nuts.

Hex nut
Standard type of nut.

Nylon-insert locknut
Holds bolt tightly in place.

Acorn nut
Decorative nut, used where appearance counts.

Lock washer
Helps keep nut from working loose.

WOODWORKING ADHESIVES

For general woodworking, most professionals use white or yellow glue, but there are times when the adhesive depends on the job. The chart below lists the characteristics and uses of the many adhesives available to today's do-it-yourselfer.

Type	Characteristics	Uses
White common household glue (polyvinyl acetate)	Rigid bond; difficult to sand (clogs sandpaper); softens above 150°F; not waterproof.	Indoor only; not for high heat and moisture areas; must be clamped; resists grease and solvents.
Yellow or brown carpenter's or wood glue (aliphatic resin)	Rigid bond; dries clear or brown; heat-resistant (can be sanded); applied at temperatures as low as 60°F; more moisture-resistant than white glue.	Best for general woodworking; for indoor use and large assemblies; water-resistant formula good for above-grade exterior uses; must be clamped.
Resorcinol glue (marine resin)	Strong, permanent bond; leaves dark stain that may show through paint; can be sanded; waterproof; toxic (releases formaldehyde).	Bonds wood in high-moisture applications; must be clamped; fills gaps between materials.
Plastic resin glue	Strong bond; powder must be mixed with water; can be sanded; water-resistant (not waterproof); urea-formaldehyde base potentially toxic.	Indoor use; must be clamped; bond is light-colored and stain-free with some water resistance; fills small gaps between materials.
Liquid hide glue	Strong bond; slow to set, giving long assembly time for complicated setups; can be sanded; not waterproof; reversible (with water and heat).	Good for complicated assemblies and musical instruments; must be tightly clamped.
Epoxy resin	Strong, permanent bond; two components must be mixed; water-resistant to waterproof, depending on type; uncured epoxy is toxic.	Good for indoor/outdoor projects; bonds unlike materials; fills gaps between materials; slow-setting types give generally stronger and more water-resistant bonds than fast-setting types.
Urethane glue	Strong, permanent bond (not as strong as epoxy); single component—no mixing required; waterproof; cures by exposure to moisture.	Good for general repairs; must be clamped; fills small gaps between materials.
Contact cement	Water-resistant; applied to both surfaces, which after drying bond on contact.	Bonds thin materials to a base; use to attach plastic laminate to wood. Choose newer, less toxic water-base types, although they may warp thin veneers.
Hot-melt glue	Flexible bond; waterproof; applied with electric glue gun; bonds on cooling (glue solidifies).	Fast-setting; bonds awkward-shaped materials that can't be clamped; good for fast repairs; generally lower strength than other glues; fills gaps.
Instant or super glue (cyanoacrylate)	Moisture-curing; fast-setting; strong bond; water-resistant.	Secures materials that can't be clamped; types available to bond nonporous as well as porous materials, such as wood. CAUTION: Bonds quickly to skin.

HINGES

As with wood and fasteners, deciding on the right hinge for your project will depend on the final appearance you are trying to achieve. You can find cabinet door hinges in a wide variety of styles, sizes, and finishes to fit flush, lipped, and overlay doors. A small selection is shown below.

Hinges can be found at hardware and home centers in virtually every style and size. Try to decide on the type as soon as you begin to plan your project, as they will have some bearing on the style and function of the unit. Some hinges add to the beauty of the piece, while the value of others lies in their overall functionality.

Whenever possible, opt for self-closing hinges which don't require a separate catch to keep the door closed. If you do need catches, magnetic types are convenient—they're less dependent on strict alignment and don't wear out. See page 28 for more on catches.

Decorative butt and semiconcealed hinges are straightforward to install, such as those for face-mounted or offset doors, but other types require careful mortising or drilling. To shape a rectangular mortise, use either a chisel or electric router and template (you'll still need a chisel to square up router-cut corners).

Over the last few years, European hinges (see below) have been gaining in popularity. They're easy to install, and can be adjusted with the turn of a screw to bring a door into line. They're usually mounted directly to the carcase side and are hidden when the door is closed. And because they're spring-loaded, they don't require a catch to keep the door closed.

Once you've selected your hinges, there are four basic steps to follow to hang a typical door: Fasten the hinges on the door; line up the door and mark the upper screw holes on the carcase or faceframe; install the top screws; align the hinge and install the bottom screws.

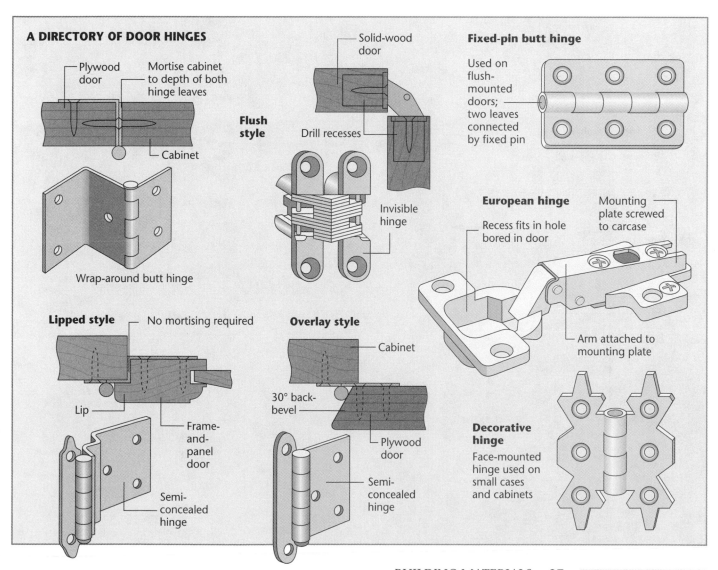

A DIRECTORY OF DOOR HINGES

Plywood door — Mortise cabinet to depth of both hinge leaves — Cabinet

Wrap-around butt hinge

Flush style — Solid-wood door — Drill recesses — Invisible hinge

Fixed-pin butt hinge
Used on flush-mounted doors; two leaves connected by fixed pin

European hinge — Recess fits in hole bored in door — Mounting plate screwed to carcase — Arm attached to mounting plate

Lipped style — No mortising required — Lip — Frame-and-panel door — Semiconcealed hinge

Overlay style — Cabinet — 30° back-bevel — Plywood door — Semiconcealed hinge

Decorative hinge
Face-mounted hinge used on small cases and cabinets

CATCHES, LATCHES & LOCKS

Nothing draws as much attention to furniture as a door that stubbornly remains slightly ajar, no matter how many times you close it. The culprit is most likely a faulty door catch, latch, or lock hardware pieces which are more essential than one might think.

As discussed on page 27, hinges alone are sometimes adequate to keep doors closed. But when furniture style dictates it, or when you might require extra holding power—such as when a mischievous child with a healthy dose of curiosity tries to get into the fine china cabinet—catches, latches, and locks are necessary.

Magnetic catches are generally your best bet. They're less dependent on strict alignment and don't wear out. Other alternatives include friction catches—where one piece physically attaches to another when the door closes—and the double and single rollers, with spring-loaded arms that close over a strike plate or screw.

Locks can be used on display cabinets to keep valuables visible but safe. Lock assemblies comprise a bolt, a strike plate, and an escutcheon, which encircles the keyhole. Make sure all hardware you choose complements one another. Some samples are shown below.

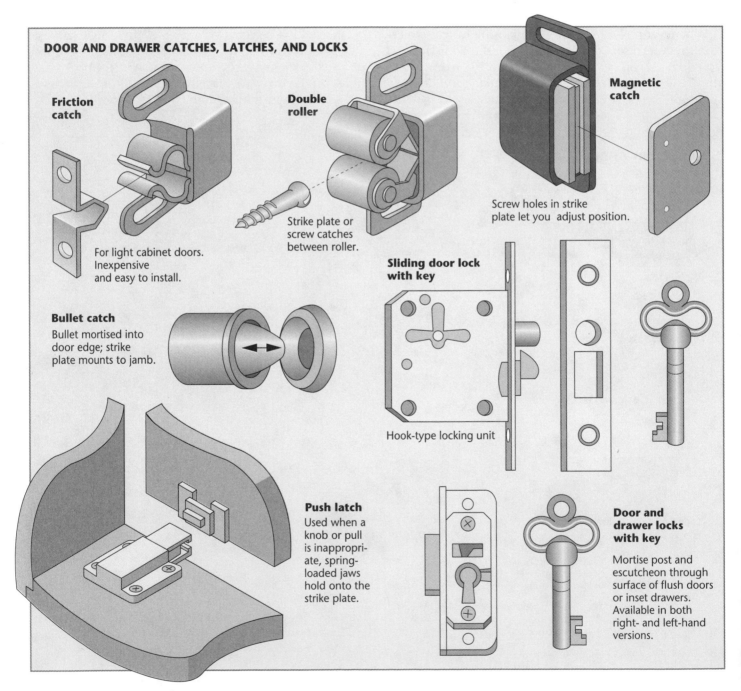

DOOR AND DRAWER CATCHES, LATCHES, AND LOCKS

Friction catch

Double roller
Strike plate or screw catches between roller.

Magnetic catch
Screw holes in strike plate let you adjust position.

For light cabinet doors. Inexpensive and easy to install.

Bullet catch
Bullet mortised into door edge; strike plate mounts to jamb.

Sliding door lock with key
Hook-type locking unit

Push latch
Used when a knob or pull is inappropriate, spring-loaded jaws hold onto the strike plate.

Door and drawer locks with key
Mortise post and escutcheon through surface of flush doors or inset drawers. Available in both right- and left-hand versions.

TRACKS, BRACKETS, PINS & CLIPS

A beautiful wall of books, vases, and hanging plants is made possible by the tracks and brackets that hold wall unit and cabinet shelves in place. Without the reinforcement that these pieces provide, your lovely arrangement may soon come tumbling down.

You can hang shelves on the wall behind a backless cabinet or bookcase, or add on to a pre-existing unit. In either case, shelf hardware is essential. You can buy brackets, braces, and metal angles in many sizes, styles,

and finishes. For both adjustability and ease of installation, manufactured tracks and brackets are an excellent choice. As well, many pieces use upright units to support shelves from the side. For adjustable shelves, use pegs, pins, or tracks and clips. Fixed shelves most commonly use the through dado.

The illustrations below show a number of different options for hanging your shelves and holding them securely in place.

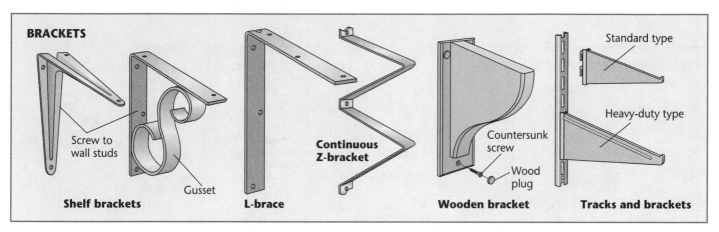

BRACKETS

Screw to wall studs

Gusset

Shelf brackets

Continuous Z-bracket

L-brace

Countersunk screw

Wood plug

Wooden bracket

Standard type

Heavy-duty type

Tracks and brackets

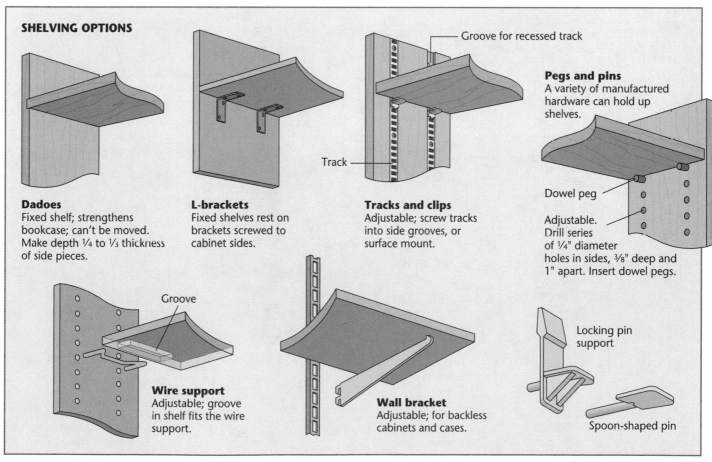

SHELVING OPTIONS

Groove for recessed track

Track

Dadoes
Fixed shelf; strengthens bookcase; can't be moved. Make depth ¼ to ⅓ thickness of side pieces.

L-brackets
Fixed shelves rest on brackets screwed to cabinet sides.

Tracks and clips
Adjustable; screw tracks into side grooves, or surface mount.

Pegs and pins
A variety of manufactured hardware can hold up shelves.

Dowel peg

Adjustable. Drill series of ¼" diameter holes in sides, ⅜" deep and 1" apart. Insert dowel pegs.

Groove

Wire support
Adjustable; groove in shelf fits the wire support.

Wall bracket
Adjustable; for backless cabinets and cases.

Locking pin support

Spoon-shaped pin

GUIDES, KNOBS & PULLS

To mount drawers and shelves in your unit—or if you choose to install rolling doors—you'll need to consider some of the hardware shown below. And once they've been mounted, choosing the right handle, pull, or knob will help complete the look of the piece; a selection of these is shown at the bottom of the page.

While guides allow drawers and doors to ride smoothly as they're being opened and closed, their appearance is not an issue because they are not intended to be showcased. The simplest and cheapest guides are wooden runners that can be made in the home workshop; the most efficient are prefabricated ball-bearing sets. These commercial models are attached to the bottoms or sides of a drawer, for example, with matching tracks mounted inside the carcase.

While guides are not important to the overall look of a unit, handles, pulls, and knobs go a long way toward adding to the beauty of a piece. There are many styles to choose from, including simple shop-made wooden creations to the more ornate types made of zinc-plated steel or polished brass.

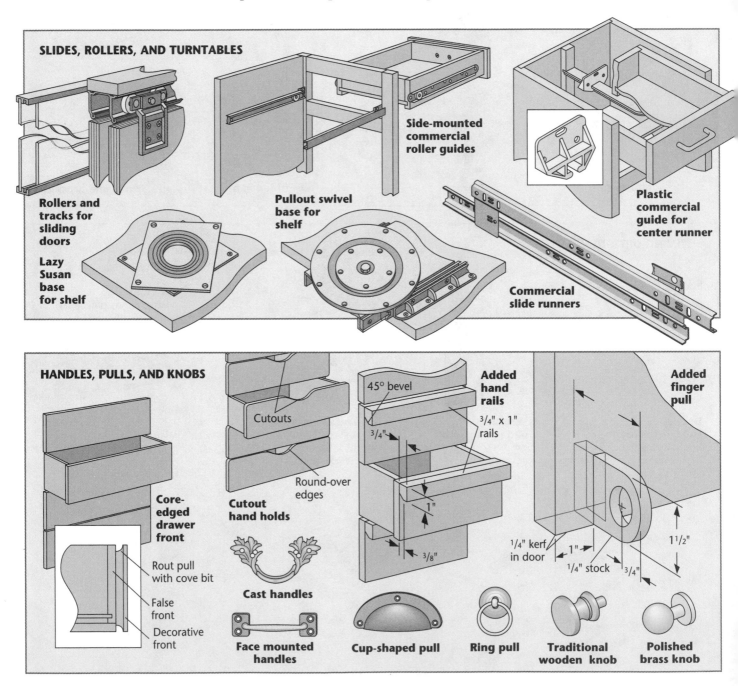

SLIDES, ROLLERS, AND TURNTABLES

Side-mounted commercial roller guides

Rollers and tracks for sliding doors

Lazy Susan base for shelf

Pullout swivel base for shelf

Plastic commercial guide for center runner

Commercial slide runners

HANDLES, PULLS, AND KNOBS

Cutouts

Core-edged drawer front

Rout pull with cove bit

False front

Decorative front

Cutout hand holds

Round-over edges

Cast handles

Face mounted handles

45° bevel

Added hand rails

3/4" x 1" rails

3/4"

1"

3/8"

Added finger pull

1/4" kerf in door

1"

1/4" stock

3/4"

1 1/2"

Cup-shaped pull

Ring pull

Traditional wooden knob

Polished brass knob

SURFACE FINISHES

It's generally accepted that finishing products of today are superior to those of the past. With the improvement, however, has come greater choice, making it difficult to select the right product for your job. The chart below sets out the basics, and divides finishes into three groups: stains that color the wood to make it look aged or similar to another wood; penetrating finishes that soak into the wood—primarily natural oils and oils fortified with synthetic resins; and surface finishes that sit right on the wood, such as shellac, lacquer, varnish, and enamel.

Because many finishes are not easily categorized, it's important to read the label very carefully. Examining the list of ingredients will help you determine what type of finish it is. You'll also be able to compare by looking at the percentage of solids in each one—better finishes will have a higher percentage of the resin or oil that gives the product its name.

TYPE OF FINISHES	
Stains	**Characteristics**
Pigmented oil stain	Simple to apply; won't fade or bleed. Can make one wood species look like another. Heavy pigments can obscure grain and gum up pores in hardwoods like oak and walnut.
Penetrating oil stain	Stains with dyes rather than pigments, so pores and grain are revealed. Similar to penetrating resin, but with added color. Produces irregular results on softwoods and plywoods.
Water-base stain	Colors are brilliant, clear, and permanent. Since water raises wood grain, resanding is necessary. Very slow drying. Sold in powdered form.
Non-grain-raising stain	Bright, transparent colors; won't raise wood grain. Available premixed by mail. Very short drying time; best when sprayed.
Penetrating finishes	**Characteristics**
Boiled linseed oil	Lends warm, slightly dull patina to wood. Dries slowly; requires many coats. Moderate resistance to heat, water, and chemicals. Easily renewable.
Mineral oil	Clear, viscous, nontoxic oil good for cutting boards and serving and eating utensils. Leaves soft sheen; easily renewed. For better penetration, heat in double boiler before applying.
Tung oil	Natural oil finish; hard and highly resistant to abrasion, moisture, heat, acid, and mildew. Requires several thin, hand-rubbed applications (heavy coats wrinkle badly). Pure tung oil has low sheen; best with polymer resins added. Polymerized tung oil also builds a surface finish.
Penetrating resin (Danish oil, antique oil)	Use on hard, open-grain woods. Leaves wood looking and feeling "natural." Easy to apply and retouch; doesn't protect against heat or abrasion. May darken some woods.
Rub-on varnish	Penetrating resin and varnish combination; builds up sheen as coats are applied; dries fairly quickly. Moderately resistant to water and alcohol; darkens wood.
Surface finishes	**Characteristics**
Shellac	Lends warm luster to wood. Easy to apply, retouch, and remove. Excellent sealer. Lays down in thin, quick-drying coats; can be rubbed to a very high sheen. Little resistance to heat, alcohol, and moisture.
Lacquer	Strong, clear, quick-drying finish in both spraying and brushing form; very durable, but vulnerable to moisture. Requires three or more coats; can be polished to a high gloss. Available in less-flammable water-base form, similar to standard type, but slower drying time; nonyellowing.
Alkyd varnish	Widely compatible oil-base interior varnish; produces a thick coating with good overall resistance. Dries slowly and darkens with time. Brush marks and dust can be a problem.
Phenolic-resin varnish (spar varnish)	Tough, exterior varnish with excellent weathering resistance; flexes with wood's seasonal changes. To avoid yellowing, product should contain ultraviolet absorbers.
Polyurethane varnish	Thick, plastic, irreversible coating; nearly impervious to water, heat, and alcohol. Dries overnight. Incompatible with some stains and sealers. Follow label instructions to ensure good bonding between coats. Water-base type less resistant than solvent type.
Water-base varnish	Water base makes for easy cleanup but raises wood grain. Not as heat- or water-resistant as alkyd varnish, nor as chemical-resistant as polyurethane.
Enamel	Available in flat, semigloss, and gloss finishes in wide range of colors. May have lacquer or varnish (alkyd, polyurethane, or acrylic) base; each shares qualities as same type of clear finish.
Wax	Occasionally used as a finish, but more often applied over harder top coats. Increases luster of wood. Not very durable, but offers some protection against liquids when renewed frequently.

TOOLS AND TECHNIQUES

The lumber has been chosen. The project idea is firmly rooted in your mind. And the necessary time has been set aside for the work. Now it's time to get down to business and build. But before you do, you'll need to be familiar with the tools you will be using, the best ways to use them, and the proper safety precautions to keep in mind.

In this chapter you'll learn about the basic procedures for assembling a piece of furniture, from measuring and marking to applying a finish. As with other crafts, woodworking offers almost infinite possibilities for the builder or maker. There are numerous ways, for example, to perform any one task. The techniques shown in this chapter were chosen for their simplicity and ease of mastery. They should help you with any cabinet or bookcase you intend to build.

Even if you have done some woodworking before, take some time to review the techniques shown in this chapter. It's better to mar a few pieces of scrap wood practicing your skills than risk damaging the cherry or mahogany you have selected for your piece of furniture.

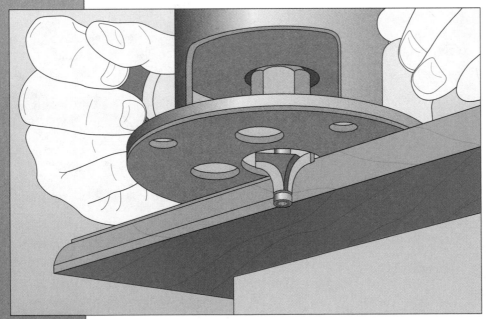

Shaped edges add a touch of elegance to bookshelves and cabinets. A router equipped with a variety of bits can produce virtually any shape you wish. For more information on using this versatile tool, see page 47.

WORKING SAFELY WITH TOOLS

Woodworking is, by its very nature, a potentially dangerous activity. The best protection is not just the appropriate safety gear but also a clear knowledge of what you are doing and a prudent attitude toward the way you work.

A SAFE WORKSHOP

Keep your work area brightly lit with overhead fluorescent lights and adjustable spotlights. Never let potentially toxic or combustible materials like paint or varnish pile up; maintain good ventilation. Keep the area clean and clutter-free. Wear protective gear *(see below)*.

Organize your tools properly. Use wall racks for small tools, and keep fasteners inside labeled minidrawers or jars. You can also build closed cabinets to keep tools and finishing products from dust and curious children.

SAFETY WITH POWER TOOLS

Always read the owner's manual carefully before you use the tool. Protect your hands and fingers from moving parts and don't wear loose clothing or jewelry. In general, let common sense guide the way you work.

Working with electricity: Use properly grounded or double-insulated tools to avoid shock. Put lighting and power tools on different circuits. A tool circuit should be at least 20 amps; stationary power tools may need a 220-volt circuit. Make sure your extension cord has the proper amp capacity to power your tools.

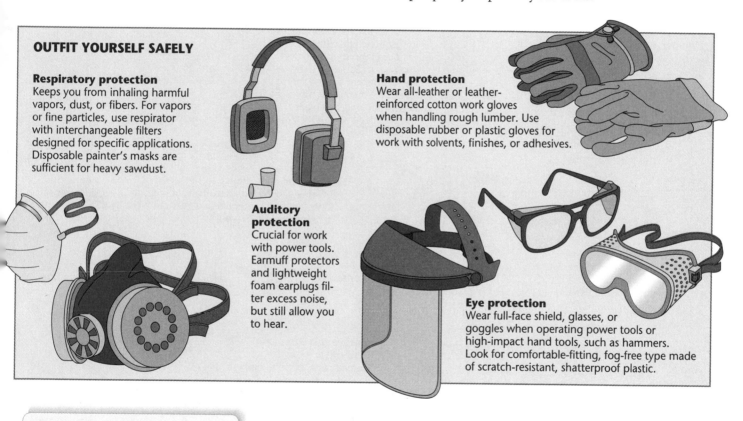

OUTFIT YOURSELF SAFELY

Respiratory protection
Keeps you from inhaling harmful vapors, dust, or fibers. For vapors or fine particles, use respirator with interchangeable filters designed for specific applications. Disposable painter's masks are sufficient for heavy sawdust.

Auditory protection
Crucial for work with power tools. Earmuff protectors and lightweight foam earplugs filter excess noise, but still allow you to hear.

Hand protection
Wear all-leather or leather-reinforced cotton work gloves when handling rough lumber. Use disposable rubber or plastic gloves for work with solvents, finishes, or adhesives.

Eye protection
Wear full-face shield, glasses, or goggles when operating power tools or high-impact hand tools, such as hammers. Look for comfortable-fitting, fog-free type made of scratch-resistant, shatterproof plastic.

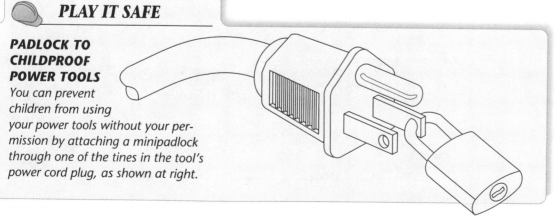

PLAY IT SAFE

PADLOCK TO CHILDPROOF POWER TOOLS
You can prevent children from using your power tools without your permission by attaching a minipadlock through one of the tines in the tool's power cord plug, as shown at right.

A GUIDE FOR CHOOSING TOOLS

Whether you're making cabinets or bookcases, using the right tools is essential to produce a sturdy and attractive piece. Illustrated below and on the opposite page are a host of hand tools that will help you with your project. If portable power tools are more to your liking, consider the collection shown beginning on page 36. And if you have the space in your workshop, stationary power tools (*page 37*) might be an option.

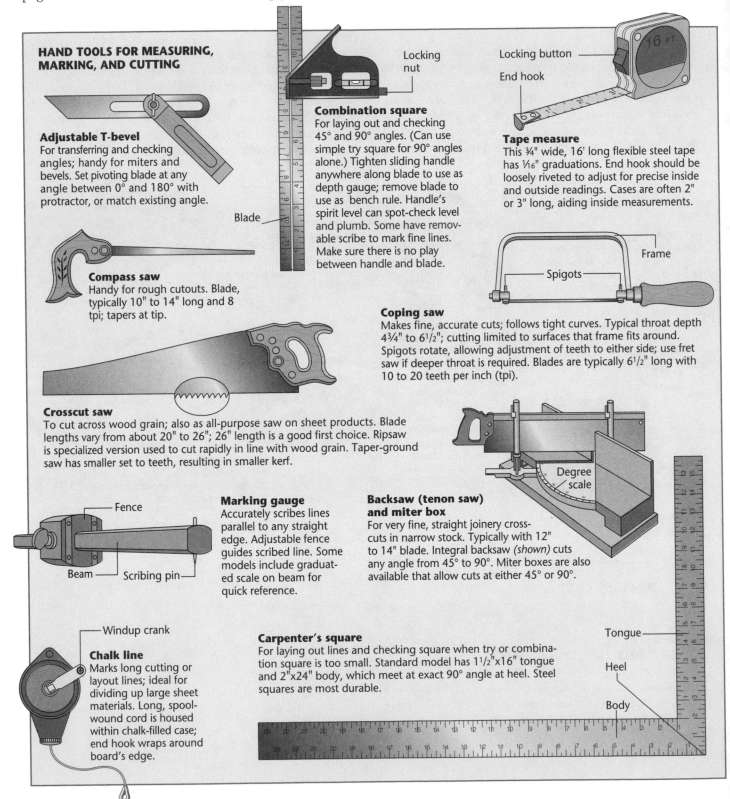

HAND TOOLS FOR MEASURING, MARKING, AND CUTTING

Adjustable T-bevel
For transferring and checking angles; handy for miters and bevels. Set pivoting blade at any angle between 0° and 180° with protractor, or match existing angle.

Compass saw
Handy for rough cutouts. Blade, typically 10" to 14" long and 8 tpi; tapers at tip.

Crosscut saw
To cut across wood grain; also as all-purpose saw on sheet products. Blade lengths vary from about 20" to 26"; 26" length is a good first choice. Ripsaw is specialized version used to cut rapidly in line with wood grain. Taper-ground saw has smaller set to teeth, resulting in smaller kerf.

Blade

Locking nut

Combination square
For laying out and checking 45° and 90° angles. (Can use simple try square for 90° angles alone.) Tighten sliding handle anywhere along blade to use as depth gauge; remove blade to use as bench rule. Handle's spirit level can spot-check level and plumb. Some have removable scribe to mark fine lines. Make sure there is no play between handle and blade.

Locking button
End hook

Tape measure
This ¾" wide, 16' long flexible steel tape has ⅟₁₆" graduations. End hook should be loosely riveted to adjust for precise inside and outside readings. Cases are often 2" or 3" long, aiding inside measurements.

Frame
Spigots

Coping saw
Makes fine, accurate cuts; follows tight curves. Typical throat depth 4¾" to 6½"; cutting limited to surfaces that frame fits around. Spigots rotate, allowing adjustment of teeth to either side; use fret saw if deeper throat is required. Blades are typically 6½" long with 10 to 20 teeth per inch (tpi).

Fence
Beam
Scribing pin

Marking gauge
Accurately scribes lines parallel to any straight edge. Adjustable fence guides scribed line. Some models include graduated scale on beam for quick reference.

Backsaw (tenon saw) and miter box
For very fine, straight joinery crosscuts in narrow stock. Typically with 12" to 14" blade. Integral backsaw (*shown*) cuts any angle from 45° to 90°. Miter boxes are also available that allow cuts at either 45° or 90°.

Degree scale

Tongue
Heel
Body

Windup crank

Chalk line
Marks long cutting or layout lines; ideal for dividing up large sheet materials. Long, spool-wound cord is housed within chalk-filled case; end hook wraps around board's edge.

Carpenter's square
For laying out lines and checking square when try or combination square is too small. Standard model has 1½"x16" tongue and 2"x24" body, which meet at exact 90° angle at heel. Steel squares are most durable.

HAND TOOLS FOR SHAPING, FASTENING AND FINISHING

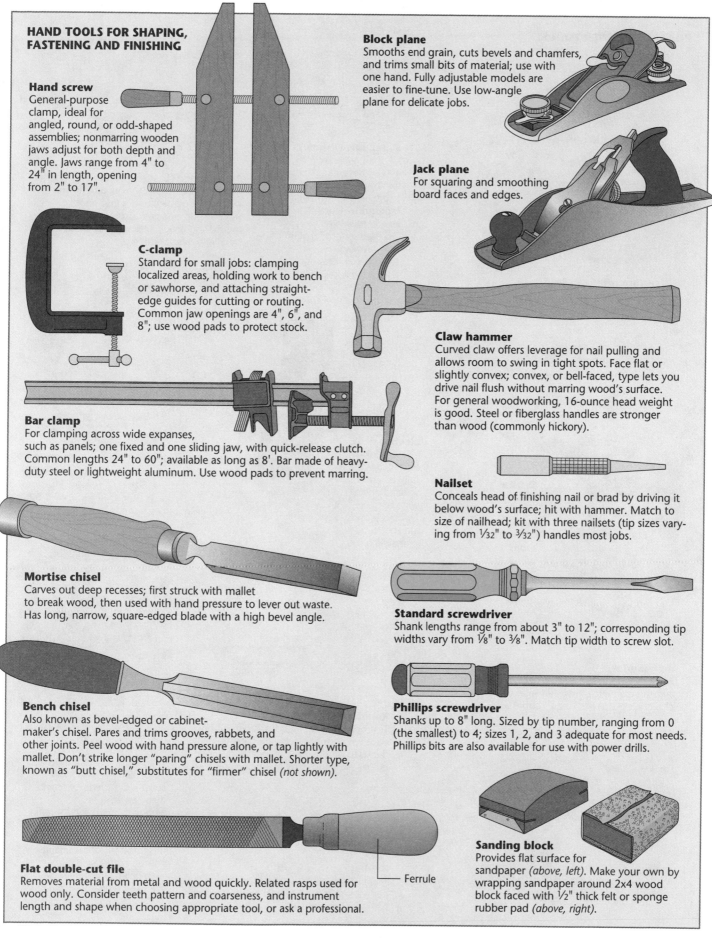

Hand screw
General-purpose clamp, ideal for angled, round, or odd-shaped assemblies; nonmarring wooden jaws adjust for both depth and angle. Jaws range from 4" to 24" in length, opening from 2" to 17".

C-clamp
Standard for small jobs: clamping localized areas, holding work to bench or sawhorse, and attaching straight-edge guides for cutting or routing. Common jaw openings are 4", 6", and 8"; use wood pads to protect stock.

Bar clamp
For clamping across wide expanses, such as panels; one fixed and one sliding jaw, with quick-release clutch. Common lengths 24" to 60"; available as long as 8'. Bar made of heavy-duty steel or lightweight aluminum. Use wood pads to prevent marring.

Mortise chisel
Carves out deep recesses; first struck with mallet to break wood, then used with hand pressure to lever out waste. Has long, narrow, square-edged blade with a high bevel angle.

Bench chisel
Also known as bevel-edged or cabinet-maker's chisel. Pares and trims grooves, rabbets, and other joints. Peel wood with hand pressure alone, or tap lightly with mallet. Don't strike longer "paring" chisels with mallet. Shorter type, known as "butt chisel," substitutes for "firmer" chisel (*not shown*).

Flat double-cut file
Removes material from metal and wood quickly. Related rasps used for wood only. Consider teeth pattern and coarseness, and instrument length and shape when choosing appropriate tool, or ask a professional.

Ferrule

Block plane
Smooths end grain, cuts bevels and chamfers, and trims small bits of material; use with one hand. Fully adjustable models are easier to fine-tune. Use low-angle plane for delicate jobs.

Jack plane
For squaring and smoothing board faces and edges.

Claw hammer
Curved claw offers leverage for nail pulling and allows room to swing in tight spots. Face flat or slightly convex; convex, or bell-faced, type lets you drive nail flush without marring wood's surface. For general woodworking, 16-ounce head weight is good. Steel or fiberglass handles are stronger than wood (commonly hickory).

Nailset
Conceals head of finishing nail or brad by driving it below wood's surface; hit with hammer. Match to size of nailhead; kit with three nailsets (tip sizes varying from $\frac{1}{32}$" to $\frac{3}{32}$") handles most jobs.

Standard screwdriver
Shank lengths range from about 3" to 12"; corresponding tip widths vary from $\frac{1}{8}$" to $\frac{3}{8}$". Match tip width to screw slot.

Phillips screwdriver
Shanks up to 8" long. Sized by tip number, ranging from 0 (the smallest) to 4; sizes 1, 2, and 3 adequate for most needs. Phillips bits are also available for use with power drills.

Sanding block
Provides flat surface for sandpaper (*above, left*). Make your own by wrapping sandpaper around 2x4 wood block faced with $\frac{1}{2}$" thick felt or sponge rubber pad (*above, right*).

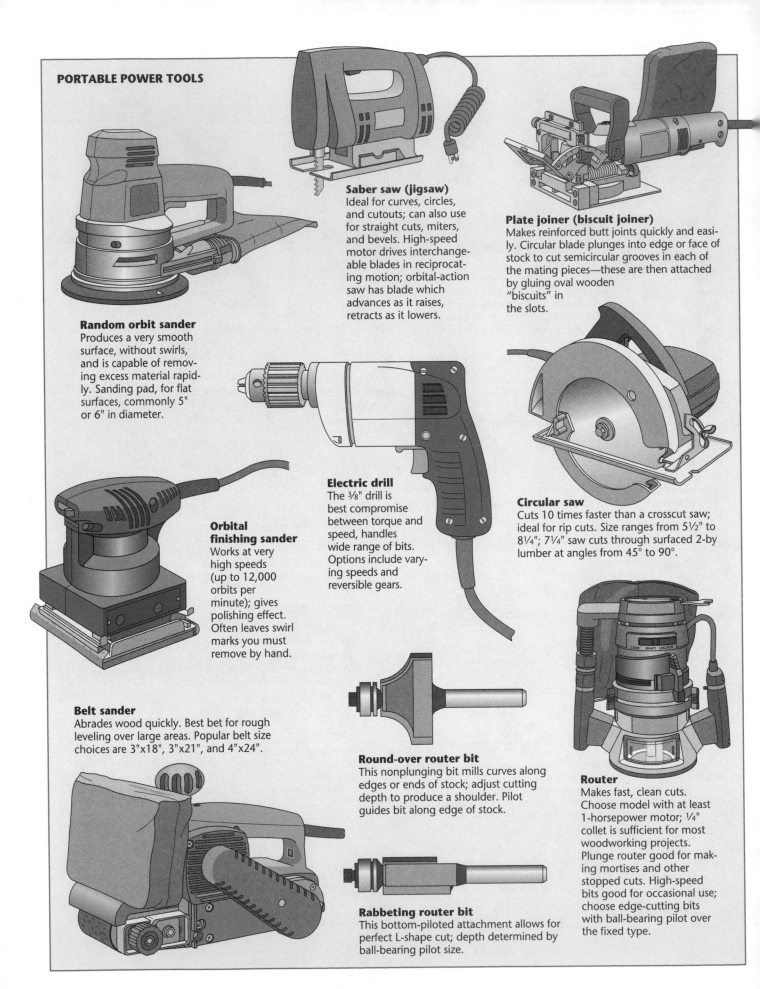

Saber saw (jigsaw)
Ideal for curves, circles, and cutouts; can also use for straight cuts, miters, and bevels. High-speed motor drives interchangeable blades in reciprocating motion; orbital-action saw has blade which advances as it raises, retracts as it lowers.

Plate joiner (biscuit joiner)
Makes reinforced butt joints quickly and easily. Circular blade plunges into edge or face of stock to cut semicircular grooves in each of the mating pieces—these are then attached by gluing oval wooden "biscuits" in the slots.

Random orbit sander
Produces a very smooth surface, without swirls, and is capable of removing excess material rapidly. Sanding pad, for flat surfaces, commonly 5" or 6" in diameter.

Orbital finishing sander
Works at very high speeds (up to 12,000 orbits per minute); gives polishing effect. Often leaves swirl marks you must remove by hand.

Electric drill
The ⅜" drill is best compromise between torque and speed, handles wide range of bits. Options include varying speeds and reversible gears.

Circular saw
Cuts 10 times faster than a crosscut saw; ideal for rip cuts. Size ranges from 5½" to 8¼"; 7¼" saw cuts through surfaced 2-by lumber at angles from 45° to 90°.

Belt sander
Abrades wood quickly. Best bet for rough leveling over large areas. Popular belt size choices are 3"x18", 3"x21", and 4"x24".

Round-over router bit
This nonplunging bit mills curves along edges or ends of stock; adjust cutting depth to produce a shoulder. Pilot guides bit along edge of stock.

Rabbeting router bit
This bottom-piloted attachment allows for perfect L-shape cut; depth determined by ball-bearing pilot size.

Router
Makes fast, clean cuts. Choose model with at least 1-horsepower motor; ¼" collet is sufficient for most woodworking projects. Plunge router good for making mortises and other stopped cuts. High-speed bits good for occasional use; choose edge-cutting bits with ball-bearing pilot over the fixed type.

STATIONARY POWER TOOLS

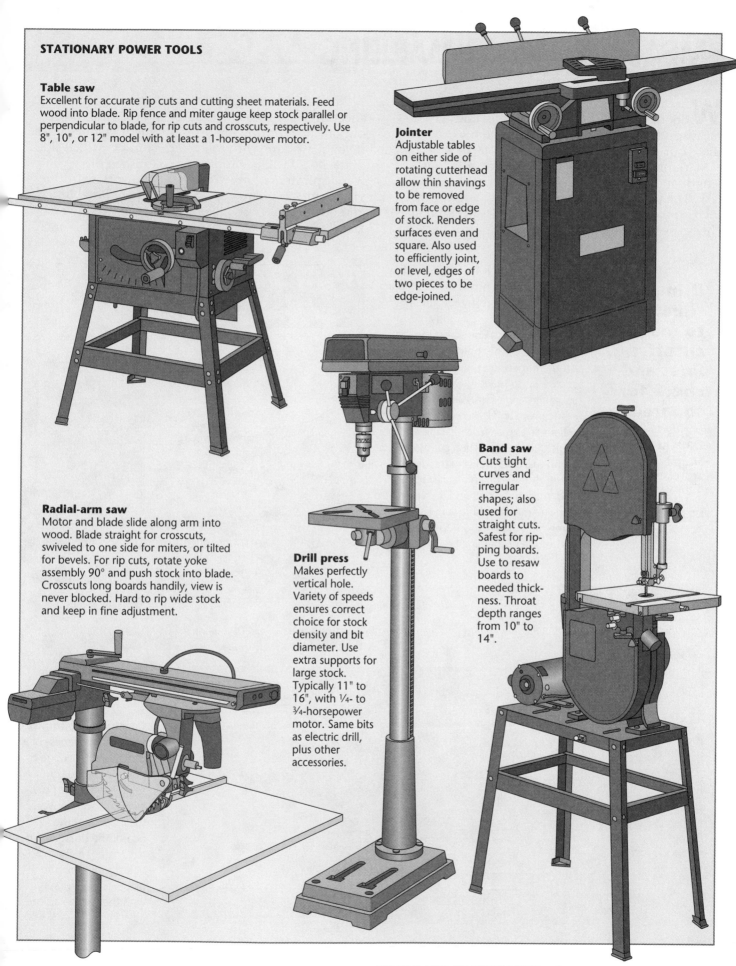

Table saw
Excellent for accurate rip cuts and cutting sheet materials. Feed wood into blade. Rip fence and miter gauge keep stock parallel or perpendicular to blade, for rip cuts and crosscuts, respectively. Use 8", 10", or 12" model with at least a 1-horsepower motor.

Jointer
Adjustable tables on either side of rotating cutterhead allow thin shavings to be removed from face or edge of stock. Renders surfaces even and square. Also used to efficiently joint, or level, edges of two pieces to be edge-joined.

Radial-arm saw
Motor and blade slide along arm into wood. Blade straight for crosscuts, swiveled to one side for miters, or tilted for bevels. For rip cuts, rotate yoke assembly 90° and push stock into blade. Crosscuts long boards handily, view is never blocked. Hard to rip wide stock and keep in fine adjustment.

Drill press
Makes perfectly vertical hole. Variety of speeds ensures correct choice for stock density and bit diameter. Use extra supports for large stock. Typically 11" to 16", with ¼- to ¾-horsepower motor. Same bits as electric drill, plus other accessories.

Band saw
Cuts tight curves and irregular shapes; also used for straight cuts. Safest for ripping boards. Use to resaw boards to needed thickness. Throat depth ranges from 10" to 14".

MEASURING AND MARKING

Whether you're constructing a basic case, adding a door, or attaching shelves, careful and accurate measuring and marking are essential to making sure that your project gets off to the right start.

Marking cutoff lines—length lines on solid boards, or length and width lines on sheet materials—is a primary task. The techniques for both are shown on the following two pages. If you are working with sheet products, check the squareness and the dimensions of the sheet.

Although factory edges are usually true, a plywood sheet may not measure exactly 4x8 feet and may be out of square, throwing off subsequent layout marks. If you're working with solid stock consider which side of the board will be visible on the finished piece. Since wood splinters where saw teeth exit, work with the visual side up if cutting with a handsaw or table saw and down for a portable power saw cut. In any case, keep in mind the old adage: "Measure twice, cut once."

Using a square to mark cutoff lines and check for squareness

TOOLKIT
• Sharp pencil or scribing tool
• Combination or try square
• Measuring tape

Marking length lines on lumber
When marking a board to be cut to a certain length, start by squaring the board. At one end, beyond any visible defects, square a line across the face. To draw this line, hold your pencil on the dimension mark and slide the square up to meet it. Hold the square's handle firmly against the edge of the board and incline your pencil at a 60° angle to mark *(right)*; angle scribing tools slightly, too. Then cut the board along this line. Measure the desired cutoff distance from the newly cut end, mark the point, and draw a second line through this point, using the same marking method. Cut to the waste side of that line.

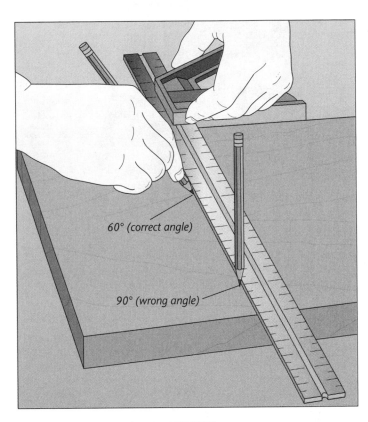

60° (correct angle)

90° (wrong angle)

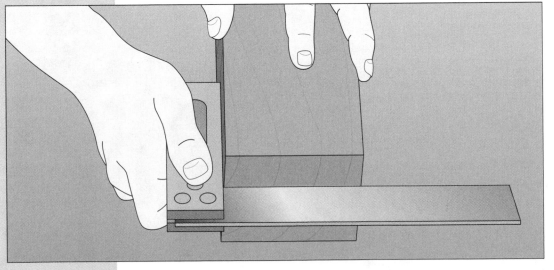

Checking for square
Test the squareness of a board's end or edge by positioning the try square as shown *(left)*. If light shows between the blade and the board, the board is out of square. To check a board's face, lay the blade across the surface with the handle on the adjacent face.

Marking angles

TOOLKIT
- Protractor
- T-bevel
- Sharp pencil or scribing tool

Using an adjustable T-bevel

To mark an angle with a T-bevel, set it to the desired angle with the help of a protractor and then use the T-bevel as your working guide. Duplicating an angle from an existing piece is simple with this tool. Just hold the T-bevel's handle against the surface that defines one side of the angle and swivel the blade into line with the other *(near right)*. Tighten the wing nut and use a pencil or scribing tool to transfer the set angle to the new stock *(far right)*.

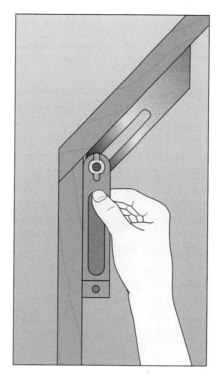 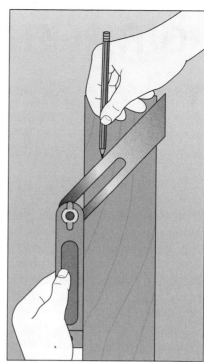

Marking sheet products

TOOLKIT
- Measuring tape
- Sharp pencil or scribing tool
- Chalk line or T-square
- Carpenter's square

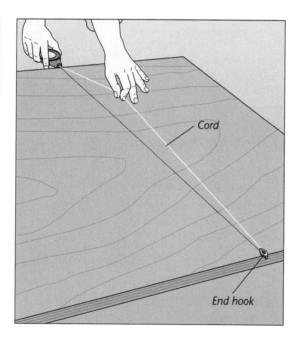

Cord

End hook

Snapping a chalk line and using a carpenter's square

Woodworkers will often do a rough layout using a chalk line or drafting T-square, just to separate the sheet into smaller, more manageable pieces. To use a chalk line, pull the chalk-covered cord from the case and stretch it taut between the two measured and marked points, making sure that the end hook is sitting snugly over one edge. Lift the cord straight up near the other edge and release it quickly so it snaps down sharply, leaving a long, straight line of chalk.

For marking finish cuts, use a carpenter's square, holding the square's tongue or body against the edge of the material and mark along the other side. For longer cutting lines, first measure along both edges of the piece, mark the dimensions, then use a long straightedge to draw a line connecting them.

Marking width and thickness

TOOLKIT
- Measuring tape
- Marking gauge

Using a marking gauge

The simplest and most accurate way to lay out width and thickness dimensions is with a marking gauge *(right)*. But before you can use the gauge, make sure that at least one face and one edge are perfectly flat and square. (See truing techniques on page 45.) To scribe a width line, set the gauge's adjustable fence to the correct distance, position the tool at the angle shown, and push the gauge away from you along the board's face. To lay out thickness, set the fence as required and push the gauge along the edge of the board.

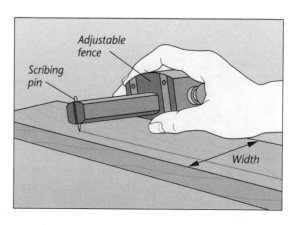

Adjustable fence

Scribing pin

Width

CUTTING STOCK

There are a variety of basic cuts that need to be made by the woodworker, including straight cuts such as crosscuts, rips, miters, and bevels. A project may also require that you make curved cuts. This section will show you how to master them all.

Crosscuts are made directly across wood grain, to cut a board to length; rip cuts are done with the grain, to reduce the board's width. A miter cut is angled, typically at 45°, across the face. Bevel cuts are angled along the edge or end of the piece.

In general, be sure the entire saw kerf is on the waste side of the cutting line, or the piece may end up being too short. For precise fitting, you can cut slightly wide of the line, then dress the cut flush with a bench or block plane.

Support the stock securely on a workbench or sawhorses. Cutting across large sheets or crosscutting long boards requires support on both sides of the cut so the waste neither tilts in (binding the saw blade) nor swings out (splintering the stock). To support the piece, bridge two sawhorses with scrap 2x4s, lay the piece on top and make the cut; thin sheets may also need support from below to prevent sagging. You'll usually need a pair of sawhorses when ripping; stop sawing when you reach the first, then move the workpiece forward or back to avoid cutting into the horses.

Curved cuts are most commonly made with a band saw or a saber saw. In general, band saws allow for more precise cuts, but there are occasions—such as when you are working with a large workpiece—when it is much easier to use a saber saw.

If you are making many repeat cuts, consider devising a jig to increase your accuracy and speed up your work. The cutoff box and the miter jig shown on page 43 are two stalwarts in the workshop and will provide you with years of reliable service.

Making crosscuts with a handsaw

Crosscutting

Hold the saw nearly vertical and slowly draw the blade up a few times to make a kerf in the edge of the board just to the waste side of your cutting line; guide the saw with the thumb of your free hand (right). Once cutting is under way, lower the saw's angle to about 45° (30° for plywood) and progress to full, even strokes. Look down the back of the tool, and align your forearm and shoulder with the saw's teeth. If the blade veers from the cutting line, twist the handle to the opposite side until the blade returns. Hold the waste piece as you near the end of the cut. With the saw vertical, make short, slow strokes to prevent the waste piece from splintering off.

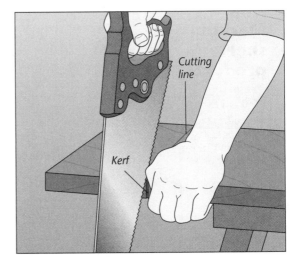

Cutting line

Kerf

Using a backsaw

TOOLKIT
• Backsaw
• Bench hook or miter box

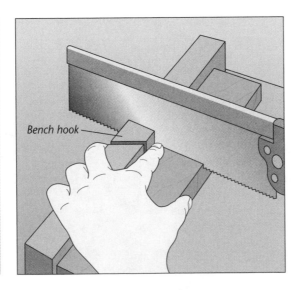

Bench hook

Making a fine cut

To make a precise 90° crosscut or miter, secure the stock in a vise, or use a bench hook. Grip the saw, keeping your arm, shoulder, and hip directly behind the blade. Begin the cut with slightly angled kerfs at both ends, then bring the saw level and take smooth, full strokes. If you use a bench hook, grasp the stock firmly with your free hand to prevent creeping. You can also use a miter box, which guides the saw at a fixed 45° or 90° angle; better models offer any angle between 0° and 90° in both directions. Insert the backsaw into the correct slot or set the degree scale, then align the cutting line with the teeth. Hold or clamp your work firmly.

Crosscutting with a circular saw

TOOLKIT
- Circular saw
- Straightedge guide
- Tape measure
- Clamps
- Carpenter's square (optional)

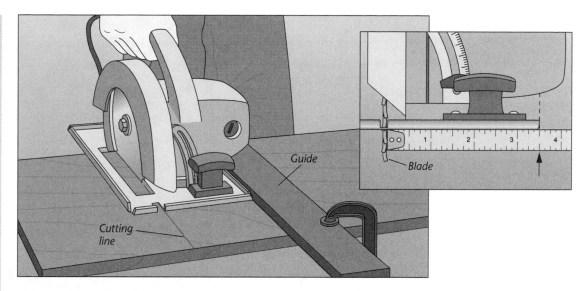

Guide

Blade

Cutting line

Using a guide board

The secret to straight crosscuts with a circular saw is to clamp a guide to the material so the saw's base plate rides against it. Use a manufactured guide or a perfectly straight length of scrap lumber, as shown above. To position the guide, unplug the saw, then measure the exact distance between the base plate's edge and a sawtooth set in that direction *(inset)*; clamp the guide or jig at that distance from your cutting line. If the saw binds, check that your support is adequate. To cut lumber thicker than the saw's capacity, first extend the cutoff line around all four sides with a square. Set the blade to just over half the depth and cut through one side. Then flip the piece over and cut through the back, carefully matching kerfs. Smooth any unevenness with a block plane or rasp.

Crosscutting with a table saw

TOOLKIT
- Table saw
- Miter gauge
- Carpenter's square
- Cutoff box or roller stand (optional)

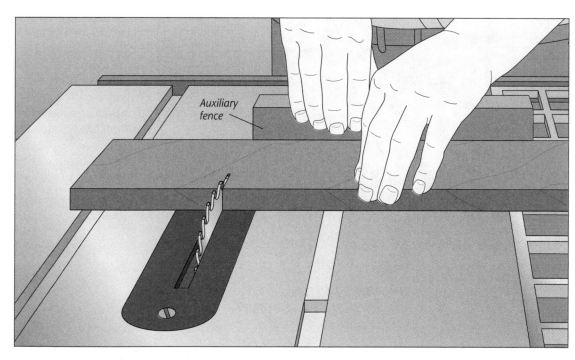

Auxiliary fence

Using the miter gauge

Place the miter gauge in either the left- or right-hand table slot. Set the scale for a 90° cut, and check the angle. Screw a hardwood auxiliary fence to the gauge to give more bearing surface for a safe, accurate cut. For long pieces, attach a longer fence. Hold the stock tightly against the gauge or fence with the left hand, as shown, and push the gauge and stock past the blade with the right hand. To cut wide material, turn the gauge around in the slot and push it through with the stock behind. A cutoff box is helpful for large stock *(see page 43)*. For long pieces, use a roller stand or a helper to support the stock. Note: Blade guard removed for clarity.

TOOLKIT
- Portable circular saw or table saw
- Ripping fence
- Kerf splitter (long rips)
- Featherboard and clamps
- Push stick
- Roller stand (optional)

Using a circular saw

To rip near a board's edge, set the blade at minimum depth and attach the ripping guide loosely. Line the blade up with the width mark at the board's end—accounting for the kerf. Tighten the fence and set blade depth. For wider rips, clamp a long scrap guide to material, or construct a simple ripping jig. To make the cut, push the saw slowly away from you, keeping the ripping guide tightly against the edge. When you need to move down the line, back the saw off an inch or so in the kerf and let the blade stop while you move. On long rips, use a kerf splitter to prevent binding and kickback *(right)*.

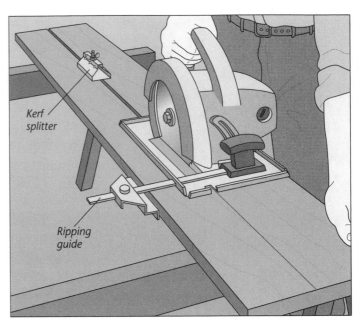

Kerf splitter

Ripping guide

Rip fence

Featherboard

Push stick

Using a table saw

A rip cut is guided by the rip fence placed on either side of the blade. Set the rip fence to the desired width by placing the stock on the table; lining up the cutting mark with the blade, butt the rip fence against the stock; lock the fence in position. Clamp a featherboard to the table in line with the front of the blade. When ripping long boards or sheet materials, you'll need a helper or other type of support, such as a roller stand at the rear of the table. You may experience kickback while ripping, so stand to one side while you're working. Don't rip twisted, badly cupped, or narrow, knotted pieces. Turn the saw on and, with the stock flat, hold it firmly against the rip fence with your left hand, as shown. Feed it into the blade with your right hand. As you near the end, use a push stick to keep your hands a safe distance from the blade. (Note: Blade guard removed for clarity.)

ASK A PRO

HOW CAN I EXTEND A COMMERCIAL EDGE GUIDE?

When commercially available edge guides are not long enough to support your workpiece, you can easily extend the length of the guide yourself. This extra length will come in handy when making wide rip cuts. Cut a strip of 3/4-inch plywood to an 8-inch-long strip. Then secure the auxiliary guide in place, as shown at right, by drilling two screw holes through the edge guide's fence.

Making angled cuts

TOOLKIT

For miters and bevels
- Table saw
- Miter gauge
- T-bevel and protractor (or combination square for 45° angles)

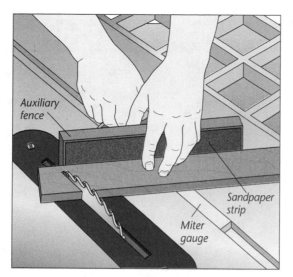

Auxiliary fence

Sandpaper strip

Miter gauge

Angled miter and compound cuts

For a miter cut, attach an auxiliary fence to the miter gauge; glue sandpaper to the fence to avoid slippage. Set the miter gauge to the desired angle and make a test cut. Grip the stock firmly and guide the gauge past the blade *(left)*. Build a miter jig *(below)* to avoid problems of repositioning the miter gauge to make matching left- and right-hand miters. For compound angles, combine crosscutting, ripping, or mitering techniques with blade tilt. Set the blade angle, tilting the blade away from the fence; test on scrap. The blade must clear both the miter gauge and blade guard. Use a push stick and a feather-board when ripping.
(Note: Blade guard removed for clarity.)

MAKE-IT-YOURSELF: HANDY TABLE SAW JIGS

The shop-made jigs shown below not only make using the table saw safer, but also ensure more accurate cuts. The cutoff box helps you make the square crosscuts needed for such things as carcase pieces. The miter jig enables you to make consistent 45° left- and right-hand miters. Both jigs run in the saw table's miter gauge slots; size the bases appropriately for the dimensions of stock you will cut most often. Make the fences from hardwood.

Cutoff box: This jig is, in effect, an enlarged table and miter gauge that provides support for true 90° cuts in wide or bulky workpieces. To assemble, place the runners in the miter gauge slots. Apply a bead of glue down each runner, lay the base on top, and screw it to the runners.

Remove the assembly from the saw table and screw the base to the fences; use a carpenter's square to keep the rear fence perfectly perpendicular to the runners. Cut a kerf through the rear fence, along the base, and through the front fence. To use, hold the stock securely against the rear fence and push the jig into the blade.

Miter jig: To make this jig, fasten the base to the runners as for a cutoff box, then cut the kerf in the base as shown. Position each miter fence at exactly 45° to the kerf, using a square to check that they form a 90° angle where they meet. Attach the rear fence. To use the jig, hold the workpiece firmly against the left or right miter fence and guide the jig into the blade.

CUTOFF BOX

Saw kerf
Parallel to miter gauge slots and through fences.

Plywood base
Use 3/4" stock.

Rear fence
High enough to support workpieces; exactly 90° to miter gauge slots.

Hardwood runners
Should fit miter gauge slots with enough leeway to slide smoothly.

90°

MITER JIG

Rear fence
Serves as handhold.

Miter fences
Two sections must form 90° angle, centered over the saw kerf.

Base
Made of 3/4" plywood.

Saw kerf
Made partway across base, parallel to miter gauge slots.

Hardwood runners
Should fit miter gauge slots with enough leeway to slide smoothly.

45°

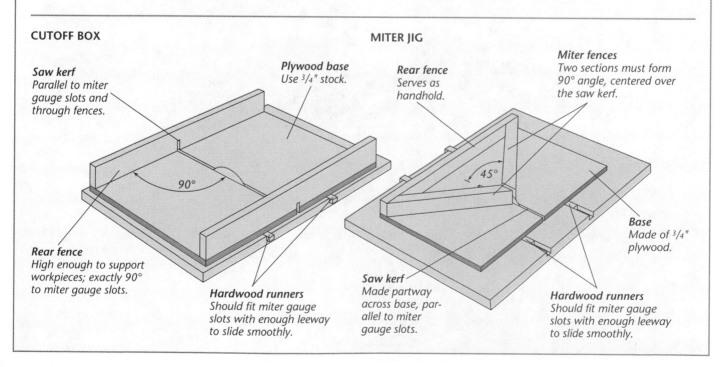

Sawing curves and circles

TOOLKIT
- Band saw
- Double-sided tape (optional)
- Saber saw
- Circle guide with pivot pin

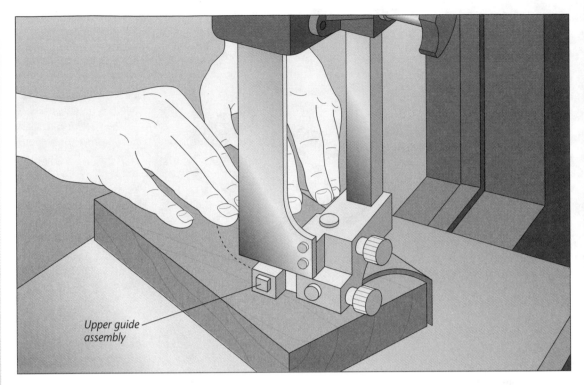

Upper guide assembly

Cutting curves with a band saw

Keep in mind that the narrower the blade you use, the tighter the curve you can cut. Set the upper blade guide assembly 1/4" above the work. To cut a simple curve, stand facing, and slightly to one side of the blade. Turn the saw on and feed the work smoothly (above)—too quickly and the blade may twist and break; too slowly and the work will burn. Feed the piece with your right hand and guide it with your left. To cut several identical pieces, join them with double-sided tape and cut them at once. For tight curves, clear most of the waste first, or cut in stages and make the second cut from the opposite direction. Cut tangentially through the waste to an edge, then continue the curve. Make notch cuts in the waste, or drill holes to the waste side of the cutting line so the waste falls away.

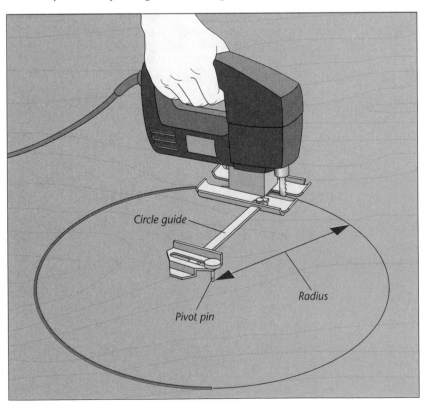

Circle guide

Pivot pin

Radius

Cutting circles with a saber saw

You can use a circle guide—often the accessory ripping fence turned upside down—to cut circles with a radius as large as 6" or 7". Before installing the guide, line up the blade on the cutting line by making a plunge cut or drilling a clearance hole. Align the pivot pin with the front of the blade and drive it into the midpoint of the circle; the length from the pin to the blade determines the circle's radius. To cut the circle, push the saw around the pivot point at a smooth and even pace.

SHAPING WOOD WITH HAND TOOLS

Once you have cut your stock to length and width, check the pieces carefully and true them. This can be done with a power jointer, but the traditional method—and one that doesn't require a considerable expense—is accomplished with hand planes. The correct techniques for using the tool to level a board face and true a board edge are shown below.

The types of planes commonly used in woodworking fall into two categories: block and bench planes. Block planes smooth end grain and bench planes square and smooth wood in line with the grain. They include the jack, jointer, and the smoothing plane. Whichever one you use, make sure that the cutting edge is sharp. The quality of your work will depend upon it.

Chisels are one of the most common tools in the shop, and yet few woodworkers take the time to learn how to use them properly. Most chiseling work boils down to either horizontal or vertical paring. See the following page for more information on the correct way to carry out these two operations.

Planing a board

TOOLKIT
• Clamps
• Jointer, jack, or smoothing plane
• Square
• Pencil

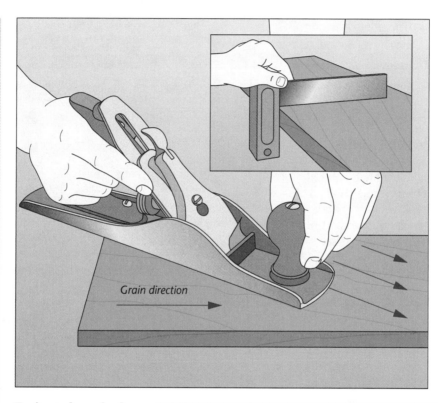

Grain direction

Leveling a board face
Clamp the stock securely. Use a jack plane; adjust the blade for a fine cut. Grip the handle and knob; work diagonally across the board, one direction at a time *(left)*. For rough stock, set the blade for a deeper cut and overlap the passes. Check the surface with a square *(inset)*; light under the blade shows low spots. Mark adjacent high spots with a pencil; plane, then test again.

Truing a board edge
Working on the edge of a long board requires a wide, balanced stance and continuous passes. Using a jointer plane, walk with each pass, if necessary *(right)*, and guide the plane by bracing the fingers of your leading hand against the face of the board *(inset)*.

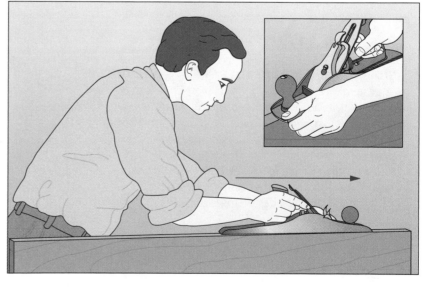

Using a chisel

TOOLKIT
- Bevel-edge bench chisel
- Clamp or vise

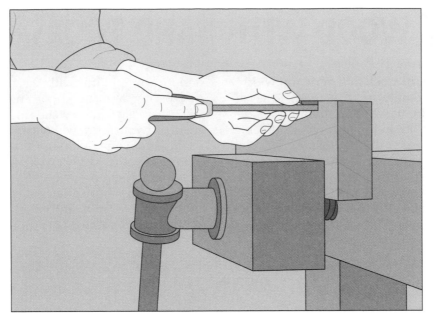

Horizontal paring
With the palm of your dominant hand against the back of the handle, grip the handle and extend your forefinger along it. Align your body directly behind the tool so your legs, hips, and shoulder can work together. Brace the blade with your other thumb on top and your forefinger below it *(left)*.

Vertical paring
Place the thumb of your dominant hand on top of the handle end and wrap your other fingers around the handle. Cock your arm up so that as you lean down, the chisel is lined up with your shoulder. As for horizontal paring, guide the blade with the thumb and forefinger of your other hand. Push down with your shoulder to drive the chisel.

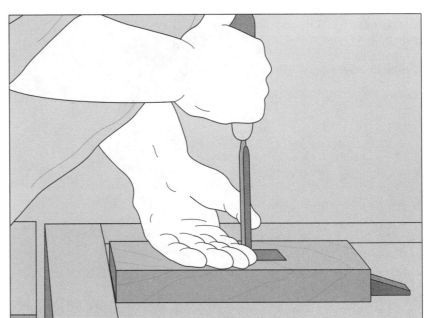

ASK A PRO

PROTECTING CHISEL BLADES IN LEATHER POUCHES
It's easy to nick or dull sharp chisel blades if you keep them loose, or in a toolbox where other objects can rub against them. One solution is to make protective leather pouches to house the blades. Cut off the fingers of an old leather glove, then wipe machine oil on the inside surfaces to ward off blade rust. Slip a "finger" over the blade, then hold it in place with an elastic band. These protective sheaths will also guard your fingers from the sharp blades themselves.

SHAPING WITH A ROUTER

With a wide variety of specialty bits to choose from, a router can perform many different woodworking tasks, including decorative grooving, joint cutting, and edge shaping *(see below)*. Carbide-tipped bits, which stay sharp much longer than steel, are your best bet if you're willing to spend a little more.

To shape the edges of a workpiece, hang it over the edge of a bench, securing it with clamps. Make sure the setup won't interfere with the router. Slip a bit into the collet and tighten the collet with a wrench; use a second wrench above the collet unless the shaft locks. The depth-setting mechanism varies from one router to the next. To ensure an accurate setting, mark the depth with chalk or a pencil on the side of the stock and lower the bit to this line. Test the setting on a piece of scrap first.

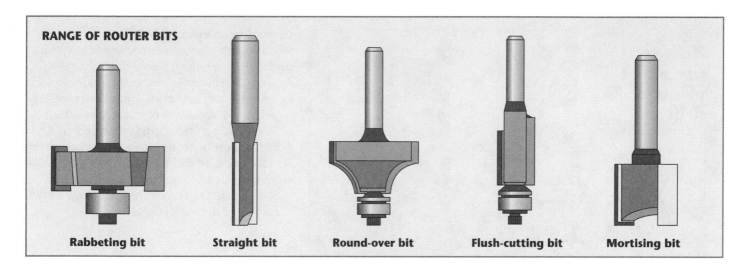

RANGE OF ROUTER BITS

| Rabbeting bit | Straight bit | Round-over bit | Flush-cutting bit | Mortising bit |

Shaping a straight edge

TOOLKIT
• Router
• Edge-shaping bit with ball-bearing pilot
• Clamps (optional)

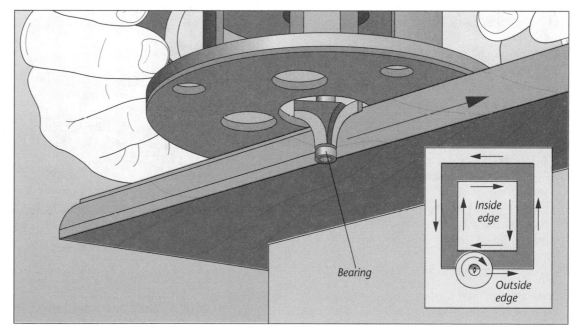

Bearing

Inside edge

Outside edge

Using a piloted bit

For edge-shaping, choose a self-piloting router bit; its bearing runs along the edge being shaped, guiding the router *(above)*. If you're shaping all four sides, begin with the end grain on one side, then continue from left to right, following the path shown *(inset)* for an outside or inside edge. If you're routing the ends only, work from the edges in, or clamp a wood block flush against the far edge to prevent the end grain from splitting as the bit exits the stock.

DRILLING

Most woodworkers use an electric drill and a variety of bits in place of the traditional manual drills (the brace and hand drill). If you do a great deal of drilling where you need precise holes, a drill press may be a worthwhile investment. In general, the electric hand drill is the best choice for the procedures shown in this book.

You'll need to drill a pilot hole before driving most types of screws, to prevent wood from splitting. Some types of pilot holes also allow the screw head to rest level with the surface.

Apart from pilot holes, woodworkers occasionally drill counterbore holes for flathead screws, or machine bolts and lag screws, so the screw heads are hidden below the wood surface. Screw heads can be concealed with putty or a wood plug. For more information on this, as well as a tip on setting screw hole depth, see below.

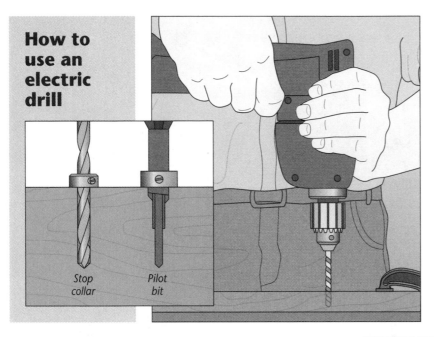

How to use an electric drill

Stop collar

Pilot bit

Operating an electric drill

When possible, clamp the workpiece before drilling, particularly when using a large drill. If your drill allows, match the speed to the job: a higher speed for small bits and softwoods, and a slower speed for large bits and hardwoods or metal. As you drill, apply only light pressure, letting the bit do the work *(left)*. Leave the motor running as you remove the bit from the wood. To drill a large hole in hardwoods—especially with oversized twist bits—first make a small lead hole. Occasionally back the larger bit out to cool it and to clear stock from the hole.

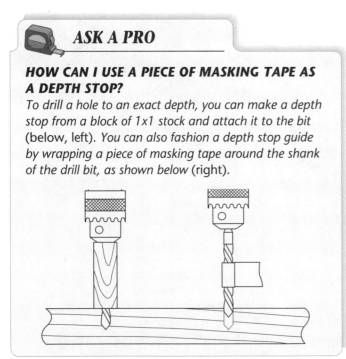

ASK A PRO

HOW CAN I USE A PIECE OF MASKING TAPE AS A DEPTH STOP?

To drill a hole to an exact depth, you can make a depth stop from a block of 1x1 stock and attach it to the bit (below, left). You can also fashion a depth stop guide by wrapping a piece of masking tape around the shank of the drill bit, as shown below (right).

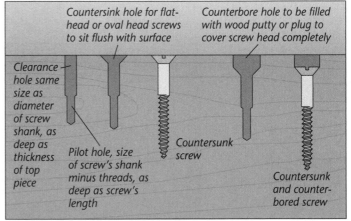

Countersink hole for flat-head or oval head screws to sit flush with surface

Counterbore hole to be filled with wood putty or plug to cover screw head completely

Clearance hole same size as diameter of screw shank, as deep as thickness of top piece

Pilot hole, size of screw's shank minus threads, as deep as screw's length

Countersunk screw

Countersunk and counter-bored screw

Drilling body and pilot holes

For a wood screw, pick a drill bit sized to the screw shank diameter at its widest; bore through the top piece to be joined. Use a second bit, sized to the shank's core between the threads, to drill a pilot hole into the lower piece *(above)*.

You don't need a pilot hole to drive a drywall screw into softwood when using a screwdriver bit. In harder wood, make a pilot hole as above. Counterbore and countersink as needed.

FASTENING

Although traditional wood joints *(see page 50)* will lend your bookcase or cabinet visual appeal, nails, screws, and bolts offer an alternative and simple way to assemble your project.

Bolts are handy—albeit less attractive—because they allow you to break down an assembly for easy moving or storage. Nails and screws, on the other hand, are far less obtrusive, especially if countersunk or counterbored *(opposite)*.

Adhesives, such as glue, are the least visible "fasteners" of all; they require that the pieces be jointed perfectly square and then carefully clamped together. Done properly, a glue bond is stronger than the wood fibers themselves.

Two of the most basic fastening techniques are nailing and driving a screw. Whichever you choose, remember that the fastener should be long enough to provide ample holding power, *(see below)*.

Nailing

TOOLKIT
- Hammer
- Drill and bit slightly smaller than nail diameter (optional)
- Nailset for finishing nails

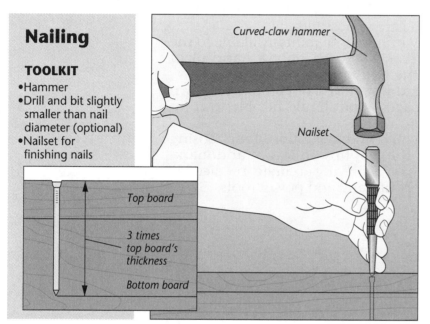

Curved-claw hammer

Nailset

Top board

3 times top board's thickness

Bottom board

Basic nailing technique

As a rule, choose a nail that's three times as long as the top piece's thickness *(inset)*. Hardwoods split easily; to avoid this, drill pilot holes first when nailing near an edge *(opposite page)*; use a bit slightly smaller than the nail.

Drive finishing nails to within $1/8$" of the surface, beginning with full hammer strokes and ending with short, careful taps. Then tap the nailhead below the surface with the point of a nailset *(left)*, and conceal the resulting hole with wood putty.

If you bend a nail, remove it with the hammer's claw—insert a scrap block between the hammer and the wood to protect the surface.

Driving a screw

TOOLKIT
- Drill and bit for pilot hole
- Screwdriver or variable-speed electric drill with screwdriver bit

Basic screwdriving technique

When screwing through one board into the end grain of another, use a screw that's long enough so that about two-thirds its length will enter the bottom piece *(near right)*. To join boards face to face, the screw should be $1/4$" shorter than the combined thicknesses *(far right)*; if the bottom piece is thick, use the two-thirds rule. Screws usually require pilot holes *(page 48)*. If you're driving screws by hand, use the correct-size screwdriver; if it's too large or too small for the screw's slot, it can burr the screw head or worse, slide off and gouge the work. If a screw is stubborn, remove it and try rubbing paraffin or paste wax on the threads. If it still sticks, drill a larger or longer pilot hole. An electric drill fitted with a screwdriver bit will save an incredible amount of time and labor. Use a variable-speed drill, keeping firm pressure and a two-handed grip on the drill to keep it from twisting or slipping as the screw slows down.

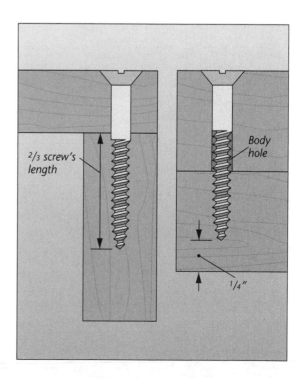

$2/3$ screw's length

Body hole

$1/4$"

JOINERY AND ASSEMBLY

The craft of joinery is an all-important aspect of your solid, finished wood projects. With secure and accurately made joints, the bookshelves and cabinets that you build will be sturdy, well made, and long-lasting. Take the time to complete these crucial steps with as much care as possible.

There are literally hundreds of joints available to the modern woodworker, but with only a handful of them—including the butt, rabbet, dado and groove, mortise-and-tenon, dovetail, and biscuit joints shown on the following pages—you should be able to complete almost any project.

In this chapter, you'll find suggestions for choosing the right joint for the job, tips on layout and marking, and procedures for achieving accurate, predictable results with a variety of hand and power tools.

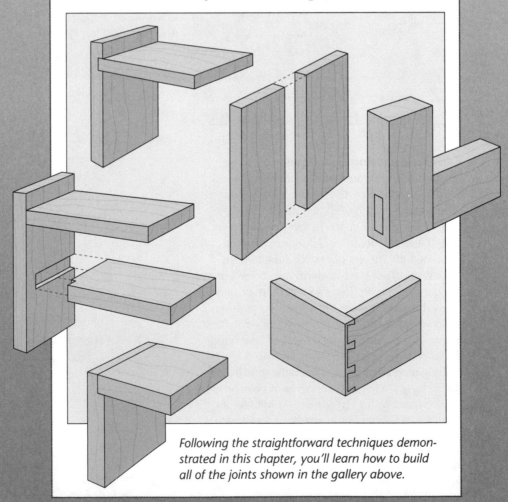

Following the straightforward techniques demonstrated in this chapter, you'll learn how to build all of the joints shown in the gallery above.

BUTT JOINTS

Butt joints are the simplest of all woodworking joints to make. Just butt two pieces of wood together and fasten them with glue or mechanical fasteners—or both. The problem is that many of these joints, such as the end-to-edge or end-to-face variety, are inherently weak, because they have minimal gluing surfaces. This is not the case with edge-to-edge joints, however. Edge-to-edge joints produce a bond that is even stronger than the wood fibers themselves. This type of joint should be used whenever you will be using narrow boards to build wide surfaces—such as the sides for a cabinet or bookcase carcase, for instance.

Edge-gluing

TOOLKIT
- Pipe or bar clamps
- Notched wood blocks
- Pencil or chalk
- Fine-grit sandpaper
- Stiff-bristle paintbrush
- Glue

1 ▶ **Setting up the boards**

Joint the boards perfectly square to ensure the strength of the joint. Lay the boards on as many bar clamps as necessary to support the stock at 24" to 36" intervals. Place the bars in notched wood blocks to keep clamps stable. Minimize warping by arranging the stock so that end grains of adjacent boards are in opposite directions. Set the stock edge-to-edge, then mark a triangle *(right)* to help you realign them later.

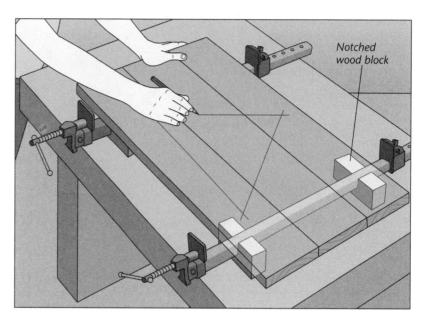

Notched wood block

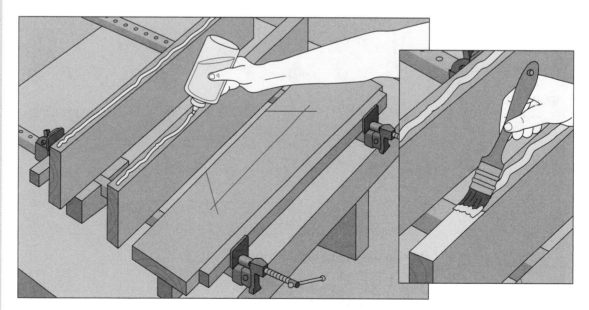

2 **Gluing and clamping**

Keep the first board face down and stand the other boards on edge with the triangle marks facing away from you. Spread glue on the board edges *(above)*, then spread the adhesive evenly with a small, stiff-bristle brush *(inset)*. Lay the boards, lining up the triangle pattern, then tighten the clamps under the boards until they butt together. Protect the panel edges with pieces of scrap wood. Add clamps from the top, centering them between the bottom clamps. Tighten all the clamps slowly, making sure all the boards stay flat and in alignment.

RABBET JOINTS

A rabbet is an L-shaped recess cut along the edge or end of a piece of wood to accommodate another piece. This joint is easy to cut and assemble. It's also strong and shows less end grain than a butt joint. Rabbet joints can be used to build drawers, form lips on door fronts, and join the sides of a cabinet carcase.

Before cutting a rabbet, calculate the dimensions for both the cheek and the shoulder; guidelines for dimen-

sions of the three most common rabbet joints are shown below. You can make the joint with a variety of hand and power tools, including the router or the table saw, which are shown on the following pages.

If you prefer working with hand tools, you can cut a rabbet with a backsaw or with a rabbet plane, but keep in mind that you'll need plenty of practice on scrap wood to learn to do it right.

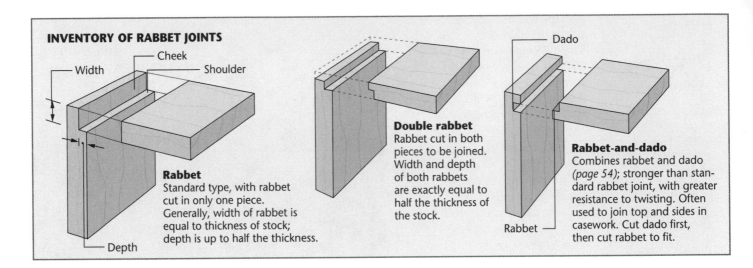

INVENTORY OF RABBET JOINTS

Rabbet
Standard type, with rabbet cut in only one piece. Generally, width of rabbet is equal to thickness of stock; depth is up to half the thickness.

Double rabbet
Rabbet cut in both pieces to be joined. Width and depth of both rabbets are exactly equal to half the thickness of the stock.

Rabbet-and-dado
Combines rabbet and dado *(page 54)*; stronger than standard rabbet joint, with greater resistance to twisting. Often used to join top and sides in casework. Cut dado first, then cut rabbet to fit.

Rabbeting with a router

TOOLKIT
- Rabbeting bit with a ball-bearing pilot OR
- Straight bit
- Edge guide or straightedge and clamps

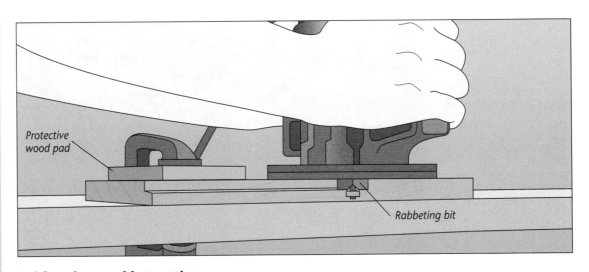

Quick and easy rabbet cutting
Install a rabbeting bit with a ball-bearing pilot to guide the router *(above)*; keep the pilot snug against the stock while you're cutting. Or, especially for rabbets wider than ³/₈", use a straight bit and guide the router with an edge guide *(page 55)* or a straightedge; the bit should cut on the waste side of the shoulder line. When cutting, keep the edge guide tight against the stock, or the router base plate tight against the straightedge. Depending on the router, the depth of the rabbet, and the hardness of the

wood, you may have to make several shallow cuts instead of one pass. If the rabbet is wider than your straight bit, cut along the shoulder line first, then remove the rest of the waste. To cut a rabbet on the end of narrow stock, clamp the wood to the bench and fasten scrap pieces of the same thickness as the wood along both its sides. Keep scrap edges flush with the board's end. Scraps will support the router's base plate and prevent the bit from rounding or tearing out at the corners.

Cutting a rabbet with a table saw

TOOLKIT
• Standard blade or dado head

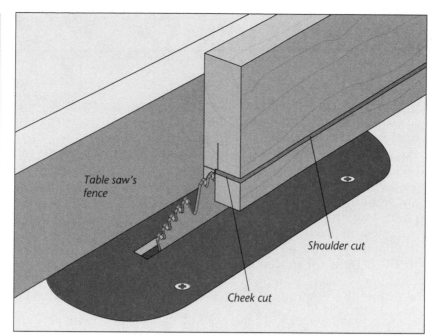

Table saw's fence

Shoulder cut

Cheek cut

With a standard blade

Mark the depth and width of the rabbet on the front edge of the stock. To make the shoulder cut, set the piece flat and raise the blade to match the depth mark. Make the cheek cut with the stock on edge *(left);* align the blade with the width mark by adjusting the table saw's fence. CAUTION: Blade guard has been removed for clarity.

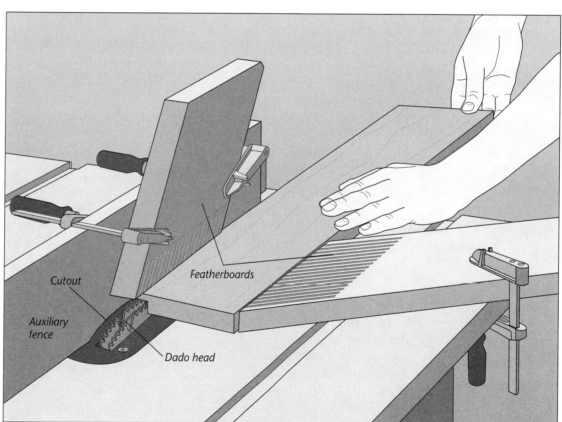

Cutout

Auxiliary fence

Dado head

Featherboards

With a dado head

Equipped with a dado head, a table saw can cut a rabbet in a single pass *(above).* First, set up the head *(page 55).* Then, to prevent the dado head from hitting the rip fence, make an auxiliary fence using a straight 1x4 the same length as the rip fence. Position the rip fence about 1/4" from the dado head and lower the blade beneath the surface. Fasten the auxiliary fence to the rip fence, then turn on the saw and slowly raise the dado head until the resulting

cutout is 3/4" to 1" high. Set the blade height to the depth of the rabbet, and position the rip fence so the blade lines up with the waste side of the shoulder line. Install featherboards, then run the stock through, using a push stick as your hand nears the blade.

When dadoing across grain in solid lumber, guide the piece with an extension on the miter gauge. If necessary, smooth the cut surfaces with a chisel.

DADO AND GROOVE JOINTS

A dado is a recess cut across the grain on the face of a board, while a groove goes with the grain, on either the face or edge of the board. A dado can also be combined with a rabbet *(page 52)*.

Strong and easy to make, dado joints are self-aligning and simple to square. Use them primarily in casework to join shelves to uprights, partitions to tops and bottoms, and drawer backs to sides. Use grooves for frame-and-panel assemblies *(page 74)* or as joints, such as the tongue-and-groove. Used for edge-joined pieces that make up furniture backs, the groove is often not glued to allow for movement.

Dadoes and grooves are either through or stopped at one or both ends. For the through type, cut the dado from edge to edge or the groove from end to end; for the stopped type, cut the dado or groove only partway and notch the other piece to fit. The end of a through joint can be covered with a facing or molding to hide the recess; the recess doesn't show in a stopped joint.

The first step for a dado or groove joint is to measure and mark the location of the outside edges. Then set a marking gauge or combination square for the depth of the recess. Mark the bottom of the cut; for a dado or a face groove, one-quarter to one-third the thickness of the board is enough (never exceed one-half). An edge groove is often 1/2 inch deep, and no wider than a third the thickness of the stock. For a stopped cut, draw a line on the face or edge of the board to indicate the end.

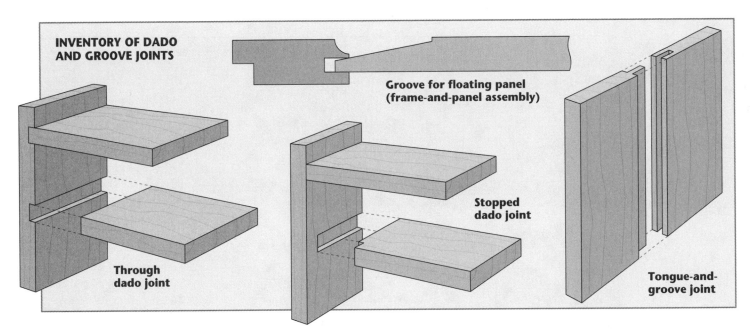

INVENTORY OF DADO AND GROOVE JOINTS

Groove for floating panel (frame-and-panel assembly)

Stopped dado joint

Through dado joint

Tongue-and-groove joint

Cutting a dado with hand tools

TOOLKIT
- Backsaw
- Straightedge guide and clamps
- Chisel and mallet

Making the cuts and removing the waste

Because of the length of the saw, this technique works best for dadoes only up to 8" long. Secure the board in a vise or clamp it to the bench. Cut on the waste side of one line to the depth line; clamp a hardwood straightedge to the board to guide your saw. Next, cut on the waste side of the other line *(right)*, then make several cuts to the depth mark between the first two cuts. To remove the waste, start at one edge, holding a chisel bevel side down and tapping it lightly with a mallet. Work toward the center, gradually lowering the depth of your cuts *(inset)*. Smooth the bottom of the dado with the chisel held flat, bevel side up.

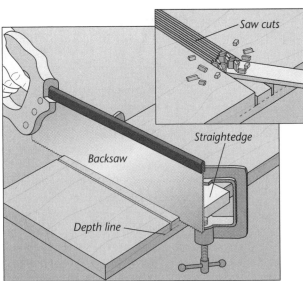

Saw cuts

Straightedge

Backsaw

Depth line

Routing a dado or groove

TOOLKIT
• Straight bit
• Edge guide
• Router table (optional)
For stopped cut:
• Clamp
• Chisel

Setting up and making the cut

Rout a recess simply and accurately with a straight bit the same size as the dado or groove's width and some sort of guide. Use an adjustable edge guide (available for most router models), a straightedge guide (store-bought or made from a scrap piece of hardwood), or for a wider recess, a shop-built jig.

For grooves or dadoes that are within about 6" from an edge or end, an edge guide *(right)* is the most convenient choice; adjust it so the bit lines up exactly with the marked lines. If you're using a straightedge guide instead, clamp it to the board at the correct distance from the outline. To cut a groove in the edge of a piece, use a router table or set up a wider platform for the router and use the edge guide.

Set the router bit for the desired depth of cut, then make a test cut on a piece of scrap wood. Make several shallow passes instead of removing all the waste at once; adjust the bit each time until the full depth is reached. To rout the recess, push or pull the router through the stock from left to right, keeping the guide fence tight against the board's edge—or end—or the router's base plate firmly against the clamped-on straightedge.

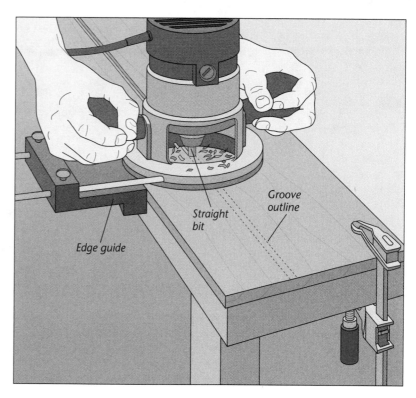

Edge guide

Straight bit

Groove outline

Making a stopped dado or groove

Measure the distance from the edge of the bit to the edge of the base plate; then mark that distance beyond the desired length line. Clamp a wood block at this mark. Start the cut as you would a through dado or groove, then, when the base plate contacts the stop block, turn the router off, hold it steady, and wait for the bit to stop spinning before you remove it from the stock. If the recess is stopped on both ends, plunge the bit into the stock to start the cut. A plunge router is best for stopped cuts; it's simple to plunge into the stock and raise the bit at the end of the cut with the router running. (Consult your owner's manual for instructions on plunging and locking the bit in the lowered position.) Square up the stopped end of the recess using a chisel.

Using a table saw

TOOLKIT
• Dado head
For dado:
• Clamp and miter gauge
For groove:
• Featherboards and clamps

Setting up a dado head

Although you can use a standard blade on a table saw to cut a dado—cutting the outlines, then making several cuts in between and chiseling out the waste—it's far easier to do the job with a stacking dado head. The device consists of a pair of outside blades that sandwich a series of five chippers. The width of the cut can be varied depending on how many chippers are mounted on the arbor along with the blades. Remove the saw blade from the arbor, then install the dado head in its place. Use enough chippers to equal the desired width. For minute adjustments, insert thin cardboard between the chippers. Adjust the depth by raising or lowering the blade; make a test cut on scrap.

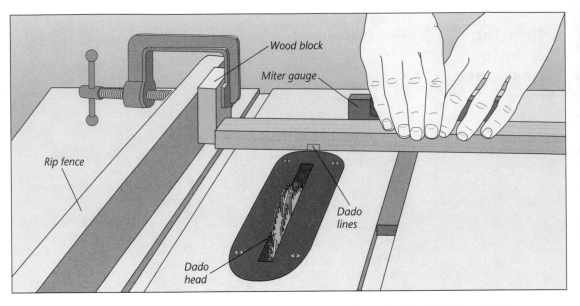

Cutting a dado

Clamp a wood block to the rip fence (near the end of the fence) to help position the stock and to prevent it from binding against the fence. Align the dado lines on the stock with the dado head, then place the rip fence so the block butts the end of the stock. Turn on the saw, and—keeping the stock tight against the miter gauge—feed the stock into the blades to cut the length of the dado. The end of the stock should pass beyond the wood block before it reaches the dado head.
CAUTION: Blade guard has been removed for clarity.

ASK A PRO

HOW DO I GET DADOES IN THE SIDES OF A BOOKCASE TO LINE UP?
When you want shelves to line up in both sides of a bookcase, prepare your setup for the first dado, then make that same cut in the other side. Then reposition the fence for the next set of cuts, and so on.

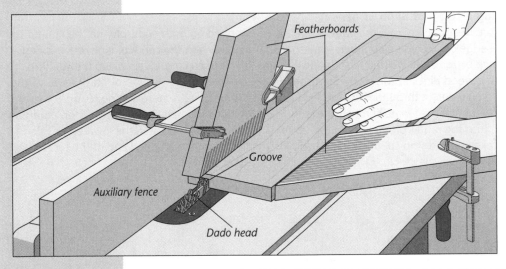

Cutting a groove

Attach a board to the rip fence as an auxiliary fence. Place the edge of the stock against the fence so that the groove lines on the stock's end line up with the dado head. Install featherboards on the table and to the auxiliary fence (left). Turn on the saw and feed the stock into the dado head to cut the length of the groove. When grooving narrow stock, use a push stick to complete the cut. If necessary, smooth the bottom of the groove with a chisel.

Cutting a stopped dado or groove

Mark a line on the top edge of the stock to indicate the end of the recess, and a corresponding line on the rip fence to show the location of the front of the dado head. Turn on the saw and feed the stock through until the mark on the stock aligns with the mark on the fence. Holding the stock still, switch off the saw. Once the blade stops, remove the piece and square up the end of the recess with a chisel; if necessary, also chisel the bottom smooth.

MORTISE-AND-TENON JOINTS

The mortise-and-tenon joint is one of the cornerstones of fine cabinetmaking. It is often used to join the frame for doors. The joint consists of a projecting tenon on one piece that fits into a mortise in another. The three most common types are blind, through, and open (*see below*). They differ primarily in the style of mortises; the tenons vary only in length and whether they have two or four shoulders.

Like dovetail joints, mortise-and-tenons require marking that is more elaborate than for most other joints. An overview of the process is provided at the bottom of this page. The steps are explained in more detail on page 58. Once the marking is completed, you can proceed to cutting the mortise (*page 59*) and the tenon (*page 60*).

The method for cutting the joint shown in this section is the traditional one with a backsaw and a chisel. Plunge routers also work well for cutting mortises, while the table saw is some woodworkers' first choice for cutting tenons. Whichever method you choose, remember that the secrets to success are careful design, accurate layout, sharp tools—and lots of practice.

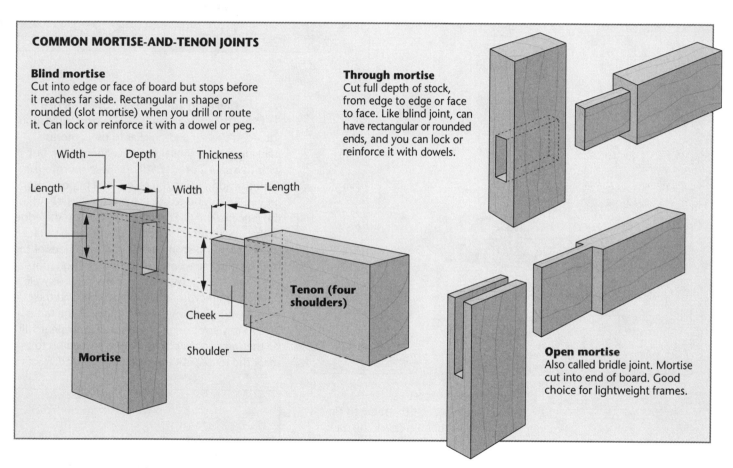

COMMON MORTISE-AND-TENON JOINTS

Blind mortise
Cut into edge or face of board but stops before it reaches far side. Rectangular in shape or rounded (slot mortise) when you drill or route it. Can lock or reinforce it with a dowel or peg.

Through mortise
Cut full depth of stock, from edge to edge or face to face. Like blind joint, can have rectangular or rounded ends, and you can lock or reinforce it with dowels.

Width — Depth — Thickness

Length

Width — Length

Tenon (four shoulders)

Cheek

Shoulder

Mortise

Open mortise
Also called bridle joint. Mortise cut into end of board. Good choice for lightweight frames.

MARKING OUT THE JOINT

The thickness of the tenon, and thus the width of the mortise, is determined by the size of the tenon stock; typically, tenon thickness, as well as that of each mortise cheek, is one-third the thickness of the stock. Cut the mortise at least 1/2 inch away from the end of the stock so that the wood doesn't split out when you insert the tenon.

In order to hide the joint line between the tenon and mortise, most tenons (except those for open mortises) are cut away on the narrow edges as well as the faces, resulting in a four-shouldered tenon (*above*). But these edge cuts don't have to be as wide; even 1/8 inch will do if the top of the tenon piece and the end of the mortise piece will not be flush. Otherwise, cut the tenon so you leave a joint flush with the top of the mortise piece.

Lay the pieces out and mark the best face of each—this should be the one that will show the most in the finished project. Then place the pieces in their relative assembly positions and mark matching sides of each joint with a letter or number. This will help you to assemble the cut pieces in their correct positions later.

Marking cutting lines

TOOLKIT
- Pencil
- Combination or try square
- Mortise marking gauge

1 ▶ **Marking the mortise length**
There is no definitive order of which to cut first, the mortise or the tenon. We have chosen to mark and cut the mortise before the tenon, because, if something goes wrong, it's much easier to cut a tenon to fit a mortise than the other way around. An alternative method is to cut one test mortise in scrap wood, then a tenon, and use that tenon to mark the actual mortises. In either case, start by marking the mortise's end lines using a square *(right)*.

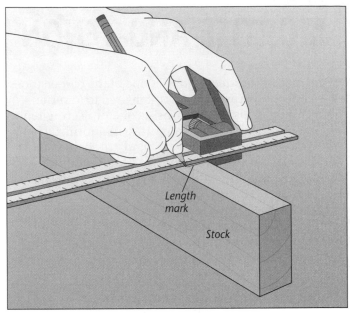

Length mark

Stock

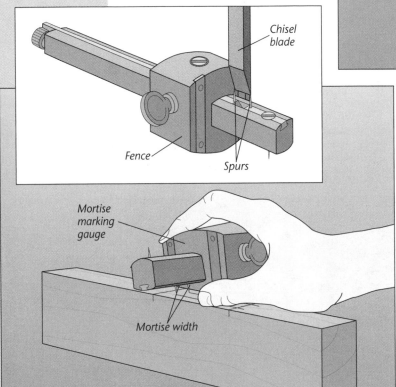

Chisel blade

Fence

Spurs

Mortise marking gauge

Mortise width

2 ▶ **Marking the sides of the mortise**
Though you can use a try or combination square, it's easier and quicker to use a mortise marking gauge, similar to a marking gauge, but with two spurs, or pins. Adjust these spurs to the mortise width, using the chisel, drill bit, or router bit you'll be using to cut the mortise *(inset)*. Adjust the fence so the lines will be centered on the edge of the stock. Place the fence against the best face of the stock and scribe the lines for the sides of the mortise into the wood *(left)*. For a through mortise, mark the opposite edge of the stock as well; for an open mortise, mark both edges and the end. Always position the fence against the same face so any error due to the fence adjustment will be the same for all pieces. Before you go on to mark the tenon, cut the mortise *(page 59)*.

3 ▶ **Marking the tenon**
If your tenon stock is the same thickness as your mortise stock, double-check the gauge setting against the mortise, then reuse it on the tenon. If the thicknesses differ, reset the gauge to mark the tenon. Most tenon pieces have a tenon at each end. Though the length of each tenon matches its mortise (it will be about 1/8" shorter in a blind joint, enough space for the glue), the distance between the tenon shoulders is the actual length of the tenon piece. Measure and mark the shoulder lines on all four sides of one end of the tenon stock. With the gauge's adjustable fence against the best face of the stock, scribe cheek lines for the tenon on the edges and end of the stock *(right)*. Cut the tenon *(page 60)*, then repeat the marking and cutting at the stock's other end.

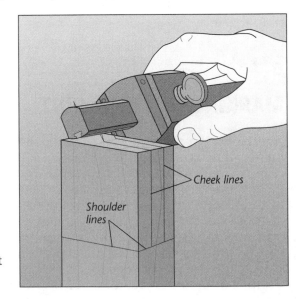

Cheek lines

Shoulder lines

CUTTING A MORTISE

Mortises can be cut in a variety of ways and with a range of hand tools and power tools, or a combination of the two. For example, a mortise chisel, an electric drill and bench chisel, or a router will all cut blind and through mortises.

Using a mortise chisel is relatively simple. The thick blade of the chisel resists twisting, and the parallel sides guide the chisel once you start it correctly. Cut a through mortise the same way you would a blind mortise, but the former goes the full depth of the stock. To make a deep through cut, mark cutting lines on both sides of the stock, so you can work from both sides toward the center. You can cut an open mortise using the same basic methods, but your job will be easier if you treat the open mortise as a simple slot, using the techniques shown at the bottom of this page.

Cutting a blind mortise with a chisel

TOOLKIT
- Mortise chisel
- Mallet

1 ▶ Cutting and levering out the waste
Clamp the stock to the bench. Cut the mortise cheeks parallel to the stock's face. Score the mortise guidelines with a chisel. Hold the chisel blade 1/8" from one end of the outline and centered between the cheek lines with the bevel toward the mortise. Strike the chisel with a mallet until the blade is about 1/4" into the wood. Move the chisel about 1/8" toward the other end, and repeat (right, above). Proceed until you're about 1/8" from the other end, levering out the waste as needed (right, below). Repeat the process in the other direction. Continue until the mortise is at the right depth and the bottom is flat.

For a through mortise, cut the mortise halfway through the stock, flip it over, then cut through from the other side. Square up the mortise ends and sides.

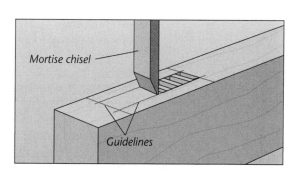
Mortise chisel / Guidelines

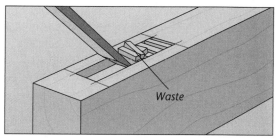
Waste

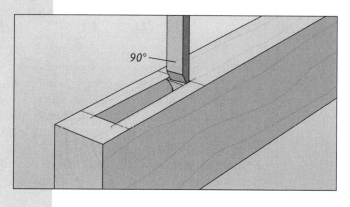
90°

◀ 2 Finishing the ends
With a chisel, remove the 1/8" of waste left at the ends of the mortise. Place the chisel blade on the score mark at one end, with the bevel facing toward the mortise. Strike the chisel sharply, being careful not to undercut the end; keep the chisel vertical. Repeat at the other end, as shown (left).

Cutting an open mortise

TOOLKIT
- Drill and bit the same diameter as mortise width
- Backsaw and bench chisel

Using a drill and backsaw
Drill a hole at the bottom of the slot from one edge to the other, making sure that the hole is exactly parallel to the end and faces of the stock. The job is easiest to do with a drill press or an electric drill outfitted with a doweling jig.

Then clamp the stock on end using a vise. With a backsaw, cut straight down on the waste side of the cheek lines to the hole (right). Square up the corners with a bench chisel.

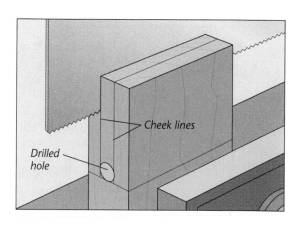
Cheek lines / Drilled hole

CUTTING A TENON

Whether you are cutting a blind, through, or open mortise-and-tenon joint, tenons vary only in their length and in the number of shoulders (they can have shoulders on two sides or on all four). A tenon can be cut with either a backsaw, a router, or a table saw.

Before gluing and clamping the joint make sure you test the fit first. You should be able to push the tenon in with a bit of light pressure, using a few mallet taps at most. Make the necessary adjustments, if any, using a block plane or chisel.

Cutting a tenon with a backsaw

TOOLKIT
- Backsaw
- Miter box
- Clamp (optional)

1 ▶ **Cutting to the shoulder line**

Clamp the stock at a 45° angle and, holding the saw level, cut to the waste side of cheek lines until you reach the shoulder line *(near right)*. Turn the stock around and repeat the process to saw the other side of the tenon. Clamp the stock upright and finish both cuts to the shoulder line *(far right)*. If you're making a four-shouldered tenon, cut extra shoulders on the narrow sides of the tenon.

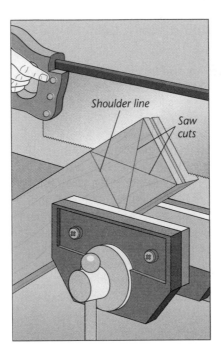

Shoulder line

Saw cuts

Waste

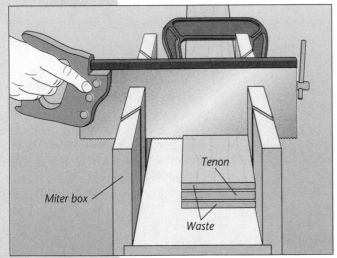

Miter box

Tenon

Waste

2 **Removing the waste**

Lay the stock flat in a miter box, aligning the waste side of the shoulder line with the 90° cut in the box. Clamp the stock in place, or hold it firmly, and saw off the waste at the shoulder line *(above)*. Flip the piece over to cut off the waste on the other side. For a four-shouldered tenon, turn the piece up on edge to remove the waste; repeat on the other edge.

TIGHTENING A LOOSE TENON

When your mortise-and-tenon joint is not as secure as it should be, tighten things up with a thin strip of veneer. (If you need more than one strip, your tenon is too loose—cut another one.) Before gluing the joint, cut the veneer so its length and width matches the tenon's. Place the veneer between the tenon and the mortise, then attach the joint. Or you could kerf the tenon along its length, then insert the veneer.

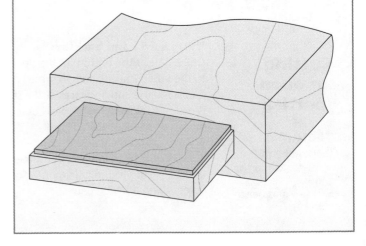

DOVETAIL JOINTS

Properly made dovetail joints, with their characteristic interlocking pins and tails, are the epitome of fine cabinetmaking. The joint is both strong and attractive. It was originally developed to compensate for the unreliable adhesives and expensive metal fasteners available in the past, but it still serves well today for joining the corners of carcases and drawers.

The time-honored way of cutting the joint is with a handsaw, a chisel, and a mallet, as described on the following pages. If power tools are more your speed, you might instead choose to use a router and a dovetail jig to create uniform, tight-fitting joints. The jig holds the two pieces of stock in the correct alignment and the router, with a dovetail bit, cuts the pins in one piece and the sockets in the other at the same time. The prices of jigs vary, but unless you want features such as variable spacing, one of the less-expensive models should meet your needs. Make several test joints to adjust the router and fixture for the cuts you want, using scrap wood the same width and thickness as your stock.

Finely made dovetails have traditionally had a half-pin at the top and bottom of the joint. Size the piece to allow for these half-pins, which can be wider than half the actual pin size. Before you begin cutting the dovetails, lightly mark a big X on the best face; this will be the outside of your piece. If you are cutting dovetails at all four corners of an assembly, set up the pieces for the best appearance and label the inside face of each piece with its name (back, front, left, and right) to make sure that you cut the pins and tails on the appropriate pieces. When you assemble a dovetail, the pins should enter the sockets with a couple of light mallet taps.

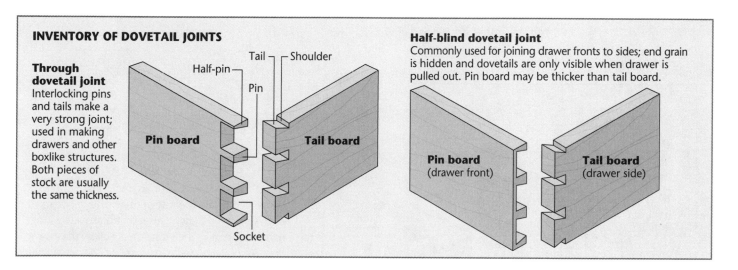

INVENTORY OF DOVETAIL JOINTS

Through dovetail joint
Interlocking pins and tails make a very strong joint; used in making drawers and other boxlike structures. Both pieces of stock are usually the same thickness.

Half-pin · Tail · Shoulder · Pin · Pin board · Tail board · Socket

Half-blind dovetail joint
Commonly used for joining drawer fronts to sides; end grain is hidden and dovetails are only visible when drawer is pulled out. Pin board may be thicker than tail board.

Pin board (drawer front) · Tail board (drawer side)

Cutting a through dovetail

TOOLKIT
- Pencil
- Marking gauge
- Dovetail template (shop-made or store-bought)
- Try or combination square
- Dovetail saw
- Coping saw
- Bench chisel no wider than the narrowest part of the waste
- Mallet

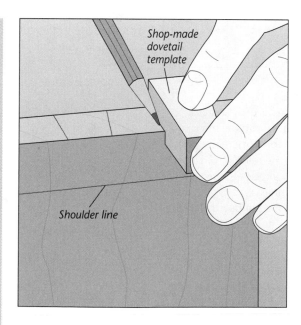

Shop-made dovetail template

Shoulder line

1 Laying out the pins
Set a marking gauge to the thickness of the stock, and mark the shoulder line on all four sides of the pin board. The angle of the pins should be approximately 80° for softwoods (a 1-in-6 slope) or 83° for hardwoods (a 1-in-8 slope). Use a commercial dovetail template, or make your own with rabbeted stock cut to the correct angle, as shown at left. Determine the size of the pins—you can make them equal to the stock's thickness—and the spacing between them. Always start with a half-pin at each edge, then space the pins equally within the remaining space. For a more handcrafted look, keep spacing irregular. Clamp the pin board in a vise and mark the pins on the end of the board *(left)*. With a square, continue these lines until you reach the shoulder lines. Indicate the waste by marking an X in all the spaces between the pins.

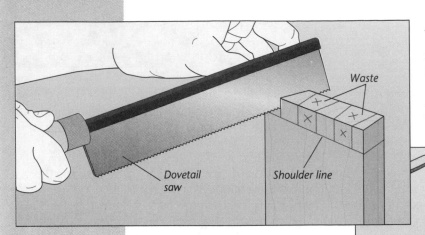

Waste

Dovetail saw

Shoulder line

2 ▶ Cutting the pins

With a dovetail saw, cut just to the waste side of the pin lines *(left)*, stopping at the shoulder line. Be sure to hold the saw perfectly vertical. Some woodworkers prefer to make all the cuts angled to the right first, then to do all those angled to the left.

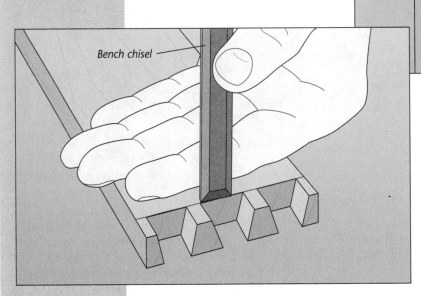

Coping saw

Waste

3 ▶ Removing the bulk of the waste

Use a coping saw to remove most of the waste from between the pins *(right)*. Don't cut too close to the pins' cutting lines or the shoulder line; it's best to use a chisel to remove the remaining wood down to the marked lines.

Bench chisel

4 ▶ Paring to the line

Clamp the pin board face-down and use a chisel to remove the rest of the waste between the pins. Choose a bench chisel that is as wide as the narrowest part of the waste area. Follow the instructions for chiseling techniques *(page 46)*, starting with a mallet. Go partway through the board, then flip it over and continue from the other side. When you are very close to the cutting lines, finish paring by hand. Make sure that all the cut surfaces are perfectly flat, and that the corners are well-defined.

5 ▶ Laying out the tails

Use the pin board you have just cut as a template to mark the tail board. With the marking gauge set to the thickness of the stock, scribe shoulder lines on all four sides of the tail board. Lay the board, outside-face down, then place the pin board on top, outside-face out (thinnest end of the pins toward the outside). Line up the pin board with the shoulder line on the tail board; its outside face should be flush with the end of the tail board. Without moving the pin board, mark the outline of the pins on the tail board *(right)*. Now remove the pin board and use a square to continue the lines on the end of the tail board. Mark Xs in all the waste areas.

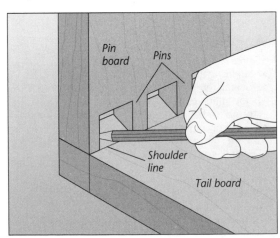

Pin board

Pins

Shoulder line

Tail board

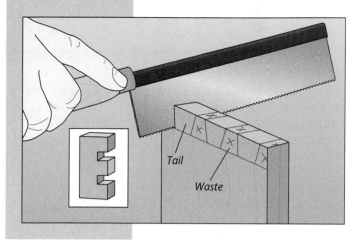

6 Cutting the tails and removing the waste

Clamp the tail board end-up in a vise. Then, with a dovetail saw, cut down to the shoulder line, just to the waste side of the tail lines *(left)*. You may find it easier to follow the angled line by angling the stock in the vise instead and cutting straight down. Adjust the board so the cutting lines angled to one side are vertical. Make these cuts, then angle the board the other way and make the cuts on the other side of the tails. Remove the waste and chisel to the line as you did for the pins. Assemble the joint, using a wooden or rubber mallet to tap the pieces together. If the joint is too tight, pare away wood as necessary. To glue up the joint, make a special clamping block *(inset)* with notches cut so pressure is applied only on the tails, and not on the pins.

Cutting a half-blind dovetail

TOOLKIT
- Marking gauge
- Dovetail template (shop-made or store-bought)
- Try or combination square
- Dovetail saw
- Bench chisel no wider than the narrowest part of the waste
- Mallet

1 Marking and cutting the pins

Start with the pin board, which, on a drawer, would be the front; clamp it upright in a vise. Set a marking gauge to the thickness of the tail board (the drawer side), and mark a shoulder line on the inside face of the pin board. Readjust the gauge to about two-thirds the pin board's thickness and mark a limit line along the end grain with the gauge's fence on the inside of the board. Use a dovetail template to mark the pins on the end as you would for a through dovetail *(page 61)*, and continue these lines to the shoulder line with a square. Waste areas should be identified with Xs. Cut to the waste side of the pin lines with a dovetail saw held on an angle *(right)*, being careful not to cross the shoulder line on the face or the limit line on the end.

2 Removing the waste

Clamp the pin board to your workbench inside-face up. Hold the chisel on the shoulder line with its bevel toward the waste, keeping it perfectly vertical as you hit it with a mallet to define the shoulder line. (You can clamp a straightedge along the shoulder line as a guide.) Repeat for the other pins; then, with the chisel horizontal and about 1/8" below the surface, remove the chip. Continue chiseling vertically and horizontally in this way *(left)* until you are near the limit line. (See page 46 for basic chiseling instructions.) Finish off paring by hand for precise cuts; the inside corners must be well-defined.

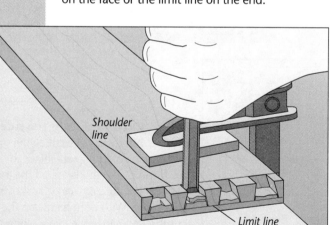

3 Marking and cutting the tails

First make a shoulder line on all four sides of the tail board with the marking gauge set to two-thirds the pin board's thickness. To mark the tails, use the same basic technique as for a through dovetail. Place the tail board flat, outside-face down, and position the pin board you just cut upright on the tail board, with its inside face on the tail board's shoulder line. Keeping both boards in place, carefully mark the pins' outline on the tail board, then use a square to continue the lines onto the end of the tail board. Mark Xs in all the waste areas, and cut the tails exactly as described for a through dovetail *(step 6, above)*.

BISCUIT JOINERY

Biscuit joints offer a highly effective way of joining wood pieces. A circular or oval compressed "biscuit" fits into slots cut in the edges or sides of the stock. Half the surface of the biscuit extends into one piece and the second half extends into the other. When glue is added, the biscuit expands and creates a solid joint. Biscuit joinery is common when attaching carcase panels, edge-gluing boards, or attaching shelves to a carcase.

The biscuit slots are cut using a biscuit, or plate, joiner. This machine is specially designed to make semi-circular cuts in the stock. Note: When cutting several slots in a row, make sure the blade has stopped spinning after each cut before moving on to the next.

Biscuit size will depend on stock thickness—for extra-large stock, cut parallel slots for two or more biscuits. Set the joiner's cut depth according to biscuit size.

Making the cuts

TOOLKIT
- Pencil or chalk
- Clamps
- Plate joiner
- Support board

1 ▶ Cutting the slots in the top panel

Place a side panel with its outside face down on a worktable, then lay the top piece outside-face up on it. Mark reference letters or numbers on the panels to help line them up during assembly. Push the top panel's edge back a distance equaling that of the stock's thickness; clamp the two pieces to the table. Support the joiner by placing a board as thick as the stock in front of the workpieces. Mark lines on the top panel for each slot so you can cut all the grooves at once. Rest the plate joiner on the support board, align the guideline on the face plate with a slot mark on the stock, then make the cut. Continue until you have made cuts at the other marks.

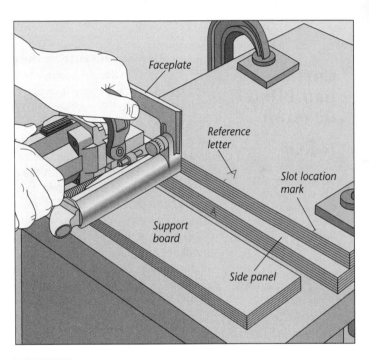

Faceplate

Reference letter

Slot location mark

Support board

Side panel

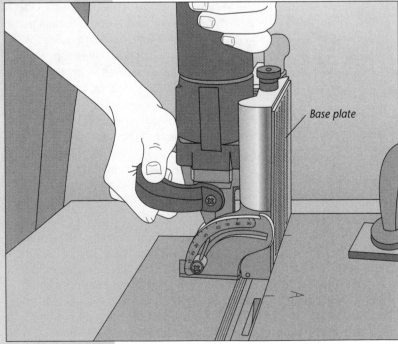

Base plate

◀ 2 Cutting slots in the side panel

After you have cut all the grooves into the top panel, hold the plate joiner so that it's vertical. Align the center guideline on the joiner's base plate with one of the slot marks, as shown in the illustration at left. With both hands on the joiner, carefully cut the slot. Move the joiner along the same edge of the side panel until the center guideline matches up with another slot location mark. When you have finished the first edge, repeat the clamping and cutting steps on the other carcase corners. Turn to page 66 for information on gluing the carcase together.

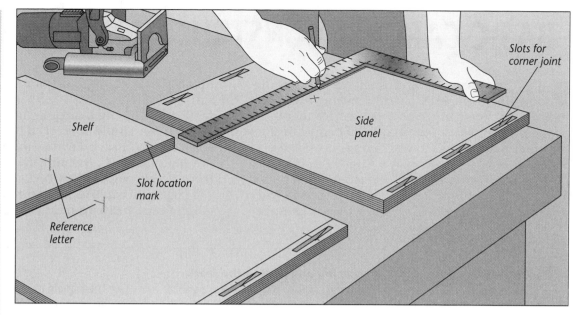

Adding a shelf to a carcase

TOOLKIT
- Pencil or chalk
- Carpenter's square
- Edge guide
- Clamps
- Plate joiner

Shelf

Slot location mark

Reference letter

Side panel

Slots for corner joint

1 Marking slots for shelves

Mark reference letters on the panels to help keep track of how they will be joined. Place the side panel on the worktable, "good" face down. Make marks at both ends of the shelf to indicate slot loca- tions. With a carpenter's square, mark the desired shelf position on one side panel, then scribe a matching line on the other. To ensure a level shelf, check that the ends of the two pieces are aligned.

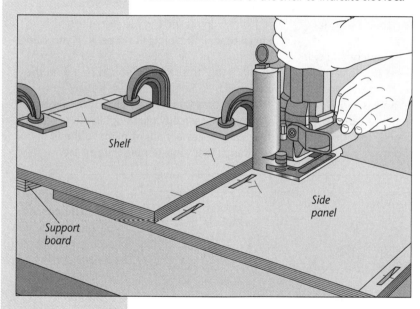

Shelf

Support board

Side panel

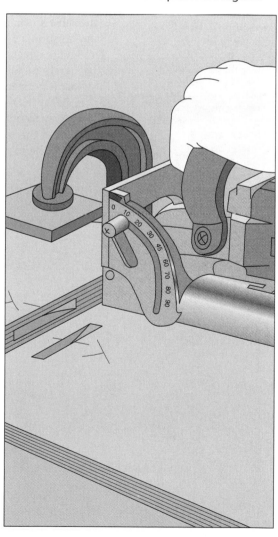

2 Cutting slots in the top panel

Align the edge of the shelf with the refer- ence line on top of one side panel (above). Keep the shelf level by placing a support board which is the same thickness as the panel under the shelf. Clamp the workpieces securely in place. Next, align the plate joiner's base plate center guideline with the shelf location marks (right) as you firmly butt the base plate against the shelf. Now, line up the guideline on the faceplate with each of the marks; you are now ready to cut slots in the shelf. Place the shelf with its uncut end on the reference line of the other side panel, then repeat the same steps to cut slots into the shelf.

BASIC CARCASE CONSTRUCTION

Building a carcase, as illustrated on this and the following page, is essentially putting together a simple box. You can create a cabinet by adding a few doors, or a bookcase by installing a couple of shelves. Information on doors and shelves is provided on pages 72 and 77 respectively.

Always keep in mind that the wood grain on all four panels should run in the same direction when they are joined together, to allow for wood move-ment; start with one side panel, whose grain should run vertically.

When designing a carcase, the choice of joints is up to you—use simple reinforced butt joints *(page 51)* for a basic look, or spend extra time and care for beautiful dovetails *(page 61)*. Biscuit *(page 64)* and rabbet joints *(page 52)* are best for plywood. As shown on the opposite page, you can use a router to cut a rabbet in the edge of the carcase to hold the back panel in place.

Making a carcase

TOOLKIT
- Appropriate tools for type of joinery
- Saw
- Sander
- Clamps
- Square
- Straightedge
- Screwdriver
- Drill and bits for counterbore, body, and pilot holes
- Mallet
- Flush-cutting saw or chisel
- Router and rabbeting bit
- Hammer

1 Preparing and joining the stock

You may choose to make your own carcase components from plywood, which is stronger, more stable, and less expensive than a series of edge-joined solid boards. If so, choose a type of joinery appropriate for this type of sheet material—rabbets or plate joints are good choices. Otherwise, select your stock and if you need pieces wider than the available stock, make panels by edge-joining, as shown on page 51.

Determine which type of joinery you will use to attach the four pieces of the carcase. In the following steps, we have chosen to use rabbets, because they are an easy and fairly common way to put together a carcase. Cut the rabbets in the side panels, to hide the end grain in the top and bottom panels.

Cut the panels to length and width, and consider whether you need to make any cuts on the panels—such as dadoes in the side pieces for shelves—before they are joined. Do this now, and then make any cuts necessary for the joints. Remember to sand any areas now that will be difficult to reach once the carcase is glued up.

Finally, dry-fit the carcase pieces together to check that all the joints fit properly. If you want, you could cut the rabbets for the back *(step 5)* at this point; this will help you in step 3, as the back will help hold the carcase square. How-ever, you may find it easier to rout the rabbet if the carcase is already glued up. In either case, make any necessary adjustments to the fit of the joints, then disassemble the carcase.

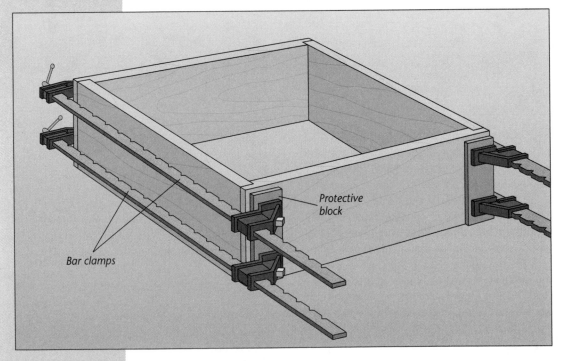

2 Gluing up the carcase

Apply glue to one side of each joint, spreading it evenly along the edge. Assemble all four sides and put on clamps, cen-tering the clamp jaws over the joint *(left)*; insert wood pads or blocks between the jaws and carcase to protect the wood. Don't tight-en the clamps all the way yet.

Protective block

Bar clamps

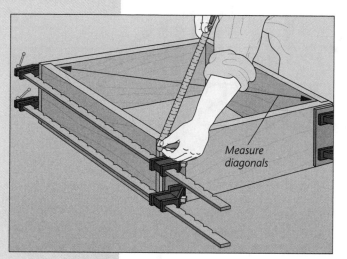

Measure diagonals

3 ▶ Checking for square

Before tightening the clamps all the way, check the assembly's alignment carefully. Measure the corner-to-corner diagonals of square or rectangular carcases: The measurements must be identical. Check 45° and 90° intersections with a combination or carpenter's square, and use a long straightedge to verify whether or not parts are in the same plane. If anything is off, now is the time to make adjustments. Loosen the clamps slightly and realign the offending parts by pulling the carcase into line with bar or pipe clamps, or shift it by pushing firmly on the long diagonal (you can use a bar or pipe clamp for this). Then retighten the clamps and check again. When everything is perfectly aligned, tighten the clamps until they're snug, but not too tight; a thin bead of glue should be squeezed out of the joint. (Don't remove the excess glue until it is dry.)

4 ▶ Reinforcing the rabbet joints

Use screws to strengthen the rabbet joints. Install a screw approximately every 4", first drilling counterbore, body, and pilot holes *(page 48)*. (With power tools, you may not need pilot holes.) Hide the screw head with a wood plug: Put a drop of glue in the hole, fit the plug in, lining up its grain pattern with that of the stock, and knock it home with light taps of a mallet. Once the glue is dry, cut off the protrusion with a flush-cutting saw *(right)* or a chisel, and sand it flush.

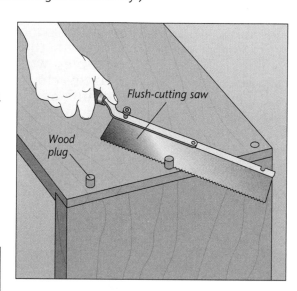

Flush-cutting saw

Wood plug

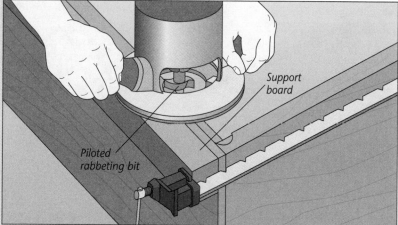

Support board

Piloted rabbeting bit

5 ▶ Installing a back panel

To provide an adequate base for the router, clamp a support board flush with the edge, as shown. Install a piloted rabbeting bit in your router; the bit should make a rabbet about one-third to half as wide as the thickness of the panel, often 3/8". Set the depth slightly deeper than the thickness of the back panel (often made from 1/4" plywood).

With the bit's pilot running along the inside of the carcase, and the router's base plate flat on the carcase edge and support board, rout a rabbet along the inner edge *(left, above)*. Repeat on the three other carcase sides, installing the support board on each side first. Then, use a chisel to make the corners square. Measure and cut a piece of 1/4" plywood to fit into the rabbeted carcase. Spread a thin, even layer of glue on the rabbets and install the back panel. Every 4" to 6", drive in finishing nails to hold the panel securely *(left)*.

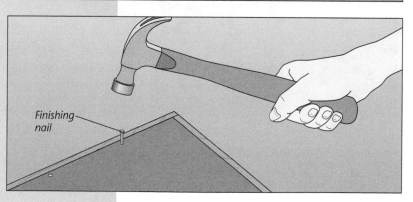

Finishing nail

DRAWERS, DOORS, AND SHELVES

Building attractive and sturdy drawers, doors, and shelves for your cabinet or bookcase is key to the overall success of the project. Of course, it's always best to decide on the material, joinery, and mounting method of these vital components during the planning stage of your particular unit. And, as much as possible, try to match the hardware—hinges for the doors and pulls for the drawers, for example—with the existing decor of the room.

In this chapter we'll introduce you to the basics of building and mounting drawers; you can find this information beginning on the opposite page. Starting on page 72, you'll learn how to cut, assemble, and mount cabinet doors. Finally, turn to page 76 to see how shelves—both fixed and adjustable—can turn a basic wooden box into a functional and beautiful bookcase.

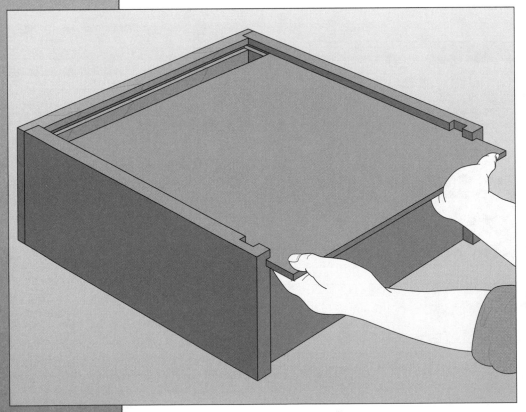

Fitting the bottom piece is the final step in assembling a drawer. For more on basic drawer construction techniques, turn to page 70.

DRAWER BASICS

Drawers come in three basic styles: flush, lipped, or overlay *(below)*. You can vary the choice of stock and joinery method to suit your budget, skill level, and ambition. The basic techniques for assembling a drawer are shown on the following page.

For drawer fronts red and white oak, cherry, and vertical-grain fir look good for a natural or stain finish. If you choose plywood, select 3/4-inch lumber-core panels, although remember that certain joints, such as dovetails, can't be made with manufactured panels.

Rabbet, through dovetail, and half-blind dovetail joints are all good choices for joining drawer fronts

to the sides. A drawer back is commonly dadoed into the drawer sides, and the drawer bottom slides into grooves in the sides and front. It's easier to build flush and overlay drawers with a false front, since you can construct the box, fit it, and then align the false front exactly with the opening in the piece.

Unless you're fitting a drawer with bottom runners, make the height of the drawer 1/4 inch less than the opening. Drawer width should be 1/8 inch narrower than the opening; if you're using side guides subtract 1/2 inch on each side. Generally, make drawer length 1/8 to 1/4 inch less than recess depth.

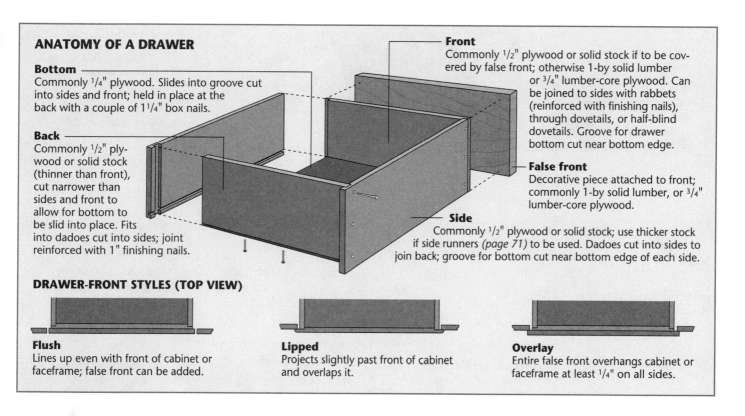

ANATOMY OF A DRAWER

Front
Commonly 1/2" plywood or solid stock if to be covered by false front; otherwise 1-by solid lumber or 3/4" lumber-core plywood. Can be joined to sides with rabbets (reinforced with finishing nails), through dovetails, or half-blind dovetails. Groove for drawer bottom cut near bottom edge.

Bottom
Commonly 1/4" plywood. Slides into groove cut into sides and front; held in place at the back with a couple of 1 1/4" box nails.

Back
Commonly 1/2" plywood or solid stock (thinner than front), cut narrower than sides and front to allow for bottom to be slid into place. Fits into dadoes cut into sides; joint reinforced with 1" finishing nails.

False front
Decorative piece attached to front; commonly 1-by solid lumber, or 3/4" lumber-core plywood.

Side
Commonly 1/2" plywood or solid stock; use thicker stock if side runners *(page 71)* to be used. Dadoes cut into sides to join back; groove for bottom cut near bottom edge of each side.

DRAWER-FRONT STYLES (TOP VIEW)

Flush
Lines up even with front of cabinet or faceframe; false front can be added.

Lipped
Projects slightly past front of cabinet and overlaps it.

Overlay
Entire false front overhangs cabinet or faceframe at least 1/4" on all sides.

Cutting drawer stock

TOOLKIT
• Saw
• Appropriate tools for type of joinery

Making dimension and joinery cuts

Make sure all the pieces are flat and square. Rip the stock for the sides, back, and front to width. (The back won't be as wide as the other pieces, to allow space for the drawer bottom to slide in; once you cut the grooves for the bottom in the sides and front, rip the back to final width.) If you're adding a false front, cut it now. Crosscut the parts to length, making sure to consider the type of joinery you'll use. Choose a front style *(see above)*; flush and overlay drawers are simplest to build, since either can have a separate

false front. Lay out and cut the desired front-to-side joinery, and then cut 1/2" wide, 1/4" deep dadoes in each side piece (set in about 1/2" from the end) to join the back. Cut 1/4" wide and deep grooves about 5/16" from the bottom edge of the sides and front for the installation of the bottom. Cut the width of the bottom 1/16" narrower than the distance to the bottom of the grooves on each side; this lets the piece expand and contract. Once you've cut all the stock to size, cut the front-to-side joints, and shape the edges.

CHOOSING A DRAWER-FRONT OPTION

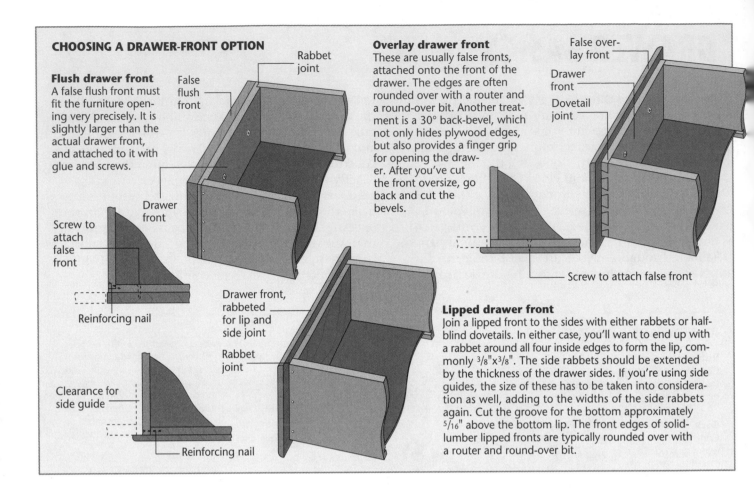

Flush drawer front
A false flush front must fit the furniture opening very precisely. It is slightly larger than the actual drawer front, and attached to it with glue and screws.

Rabbet joint

False flush front

Drawer front

Screw to attach false front

Reinforcing nail

Drawer front, rabbeted for lip and side joint

Rabbet joint

Clearance for side guide

Reinforcing nail

Overlay drawer front
These are usually false fronts, attached onto the front of the drawer. The edges are often rounded over with a router and a round-over bit. Another treatment is a 30° back-bevel, which not only hides plywood edges, but also provides a finger grip for opening the drawer. After you've cut the front oversize, go back and cut the bevels.

False overlay front

Drawer front

Dovetail joint

Screw to attach false front

Lipped drawer front
Join a lipped front to the sides with either rabbets or half-blind dovetails. In either case, you'll want to end up with a rabbet around all four inside edges to form the lip, commonly 3/8"x3/8". The side rabbets should be extended by the thickness of the drawer sides. If you're using side guides, the size of these has to be taken into consideration as well, adding to the widths of the side rabbets again. Cut the groove for the bottom approximately 5/16" above the bottom lip. The front edges of solid-lumber lipped fronts are typically rounded over with a router and round-over bit.

Assembling a drawer

TOOLKIT
- Hammer
- Bar clamps
- Glue and applicator
- 1" brads
- 1" finishing nails
- 1" box nails

1 Joining the back to the sides
Before you actually glue up the drawer, take the time to dry-fit the drawer components carefully and check for square *(page 67)*. Begin assembling the drawer with the back-to-side joints (if you're dovetailing, start with the front-to-side joints). Spread the glue inside the dadoes and along the end grain of the back. Push the ends into their dadoes. Drive three 1" brads through each of the sides into the back to lock it in place.

2 Installing the drawer front
Next, add the front (but not the false front yet). Use glue and 1" finishing nails *(right)* to reinforce the joints; you can nail at an angle if necessary. However, if you're using dovetails, glue alone is sufficient. Clamp up the drawer assembly.

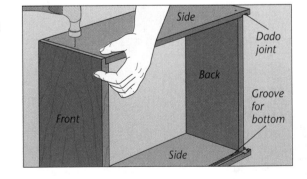

Side

Dado joint

Back

Groove for bottom

Front

Side

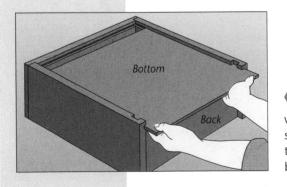

Bottom

Back

3 Installing the drawer bottom
Flip the drawer upside down and slide in the bottom *(left)* until it's flush with the back. Check for square with a try or combination square and by measuring corner-to-corner diagonals *(page 67)*. Make any necessary adjustments, then nail the bottom to the back with a couple of 1" box nails. Once the basic box is together, ease the sharp edges with a folded piece of sandpaper.

INSTALLING A DRAWER

Once you are ready to fit your drawers into the furniture, you can choose from a variety of guides, including wooden runners and the many commercially available metal guide systems. A representative sample of guides is shown below.

WOODEN RUNNERS

The simplest way to support a drawer of moderate size and load is on wooden side runners. Screw 1/2-inch by 3/4-inch hardwood strips to the insides of the carcase. The matching grooves in the drawer sides should be approximately 1/16 inch wider and deeper than the strips. Elongated screw holes let the runners expand and contract. A coat of wax helps cut friction.

Very wide or heavy drawers require a center runner. In this case, fasten a grooved wooden or plastic track to the drawer bottom; there are many ways to mount the runner, including attaching it to a dust panel dadoed into the carcase sides.

MANUFACTURED GUIDES

For the smoothest, most trouble-free drawer opening and closing, choose prefabricated metal ball-bearing guide sets attached to the drawer bottom or sides. Bottom guides are sufficient for many applications, but side guides handle more weight and operate more smoothly. Bottom guides typically require a 3/8-inch clearance top and bottom and 1/8 inch on each side, while side guides need 1/2 inch on both sides, but check the manufacturer's instructions to be sure.

If your opening includes an overhanging faceframe and you're using side guides, you'll need to bring the mounting surface flush with the edge of the face frame stiles with filler strips.

Before installing the drawers, be sure your carcase is plumb and level. Install a screw in each guide's elongated screw hole. Try the drawer out; for fine adjustments, loosen the screws slightly and reposition the guides. Once all is aligned, remove the drawer and drive in the remaining screws.

ADDING THE DECORATIVE FRONT

Fasten the decorative—or false—front to the drawer by placing it face down on the work surface. Apply glue to the front of the drawer and position it atop the false front. Add screws and wait for the glue to dry.

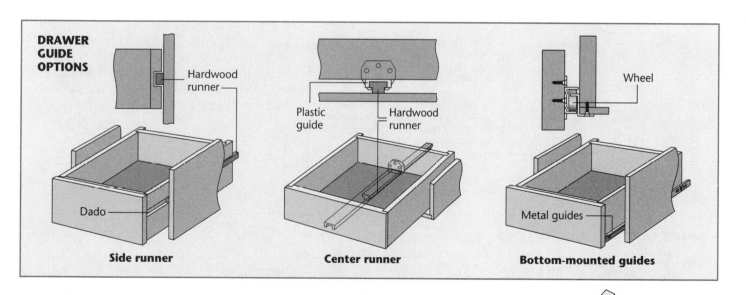

DRAWER GUIDE OPTIONS

Hardwood runner

Dado

Side runner

Plastic guide

Hardwood runner

Center runner

Wheel

Metal guides

Bottom-mounted guides

MOUNTING DRAWERS: TWO TIPS

Filler strips
Strips bring side guides flush with the faceframe. Drive screws through elongated holes and then align.

Decorative front
Screw through the false front. Oversize pilot holes and small flat washers allow for adjustment.

CABINET DOORS

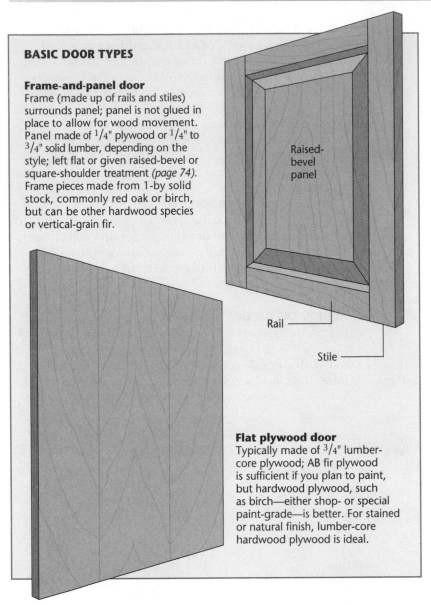

BASIC DOOR TYPES

Frame-and-panel door
Frame (made up of rails and stiles) surrounds panel; panel is not glued in place to allow for wood movement. Panel made of $1/4$" plywood or $1/4$" to $3/4$" solid lumber, depending on the style; left flat or given raised-bevel or square-shoulder treatment (page 74). Frame pieces made from 1-by solid stock, commonly red oak or birch, but can be other hardwood species or vertical-grain fir.

Raised-bevel panel

Rail

Stile

Flat plywood door
Typically made of $3/4$" lumber-core plywood; AB fir plywood is sufficient if you plan to paint, but hardwood plywood, such as birch—either shop- or special paint-grade—is better. For stained or natural finish, lumber-core hardwood plywood is ideal.

urniture doors are mostly made either from plywood (flat door) or from a panel surrounded by a frame (frame-and-panel construction), which is joined usually with open mortise and tenons, or blind mortise and tenons.

There are several ways to mount a door with respect to the cabinet face—flush, lipped, or overlay. The size of any door depends on the exact size of the opening and, in some cases, on the mounting hardware you choose (page 27). To determine the size, first measure the height and width of the opening, then follow the specifics for the different styles. Mount a flush door inside the door opening, its face flush with the cabinet or faceframe. For lipped doors, half the door thickness should project beyond the front. The overlay variety overlaps the edges of the door opening; mount it with the inside face against the cabinet front or faceframe. Make sure the overlap doesn't interfere with other doors or drawer fronts.

Frame-and-panel designs come in three basic panel types: flat, raised-bevel, and square-shoulder (see below). Secure a panel to the frame either in grooves or in rabbets; solid-wood panels should be housed in dadoes to allow for movement.

FRAME-AND-PANEL DOOR OPTIONS

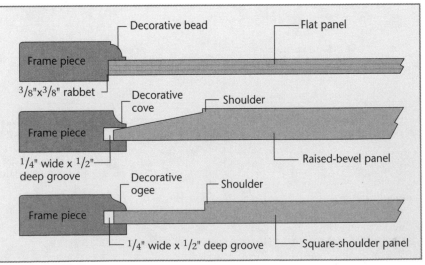

Flat plywood panel
Typically $1/4$" plywood, placed into recess formed by $3/8$"x$3/8$" rabbets cut into frame after assembly; or housed in groove with $1/16$" clearance all around.

Raised-bevel panel
Made of $1/2$" to $3/4$" solid stock; sits in grooves $1/4$" wide and $1/2$" deep cut into rails and stiles.

Square-shoulder panel
Made of $1/2$" solid stock or $1/2$" lumber-core plywood (only if it's to be painted); goes into grooves $1/4$" wide and $1/2$" deep cut into edges of frame pieces.

Decorative bead

Flat panel

Frame piece

$3/8$"x$3/8$" rabbet

Decorative cove

Shoulder

Frame piece

$1/4$" wide x $1/2$" deep groove

Raised-bevel panel

Decorative ogee

Shoulder

Frame piece

$1/4$" wide x $1/2$" deep groove

Square-shoulder panel

BUILDING DOORS

You can make doors for your cabinet using either plywood or solid stock. If using plywood, you'll often need to attach banding to conceal the edges for a finished appearance. For more information, see the steps below.

To build solid wood doors, you can choose from a host of joinery methods to build the frames. For more on joinery, see page 50. Information on fashioning the panel is provided on page 74. To assemble the door (*page 75*), you can use either solid or plywood panels.

Making plywood doors

TOOLKIT
• Saw
For flush doors:
• Iron (optional)
For lipped doors:
• Router
• Round-over or chamfering bit
• Sander

Flush plywood doors
You can cut a flush door to the exact size of the opening, with a slight back-bevel on the latch side. If you opt for veneer banding to cover plywood edges, be sure to cut your doors a bit shorter in height and width to allow for the banding's thickness. Glue the strips to the edges and "clamp" them with masking tape *(inset)*, or apply heat-set veneer tape with an iron.

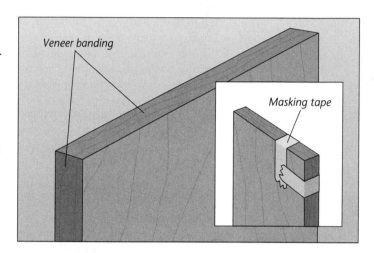

Veneer banding

Masking tape

Lipped plywood doors
Rabbet a lipped door on the back. Cut $^3/_8$"x$^3/_8$" rabbets on all edges, unless you're making double doors. In this case, cut both doors as one panel, rabbet the edges, then rip the panel down the center to divide it into two doors. If you plan to apply a natural or stained finish to the door, don't shape the front edges because the plywood veneers show up. However if you're planning to paint, you can round over the edges with a router and round-over bit, as shown, or a chamfering bit. Fill any veneer voids carefully, then sand.

Round over (only if door is to be painted)

Rabbet

Overlay doors
These doors can either be cut to size with squared edges, or cut oversize and then back-beveled about 30°; the back-bevel allows you to hide the veneers more effectively and serves as a finger pull. For best results, cut the bevels on a table or radial-arm saw, then round off any sharp edges with medium-grit sandpaper.

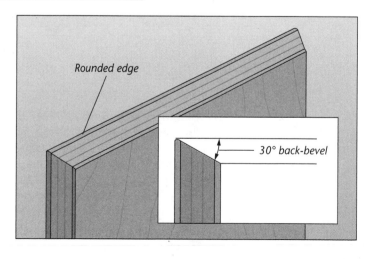

Rounded edge

30° back-bevel

Choosing the type of joinery

To connect stiles and rails that form the frame, choose doweled butt joints, half-laps, open mortise-and-tenons, or blind mortise-and-tenons. Cut frame members to size; make all joinery cuts. If joining the panel to a grooved frame, cut the grooves, from one end of the stile to the other, with a router or table saw. Cut a tenon with a haunch in the rail; a mortise is cut in the stile to receive the tenon *(right)*. The haunch fills the end of the groove cut in the stile. See page 59 for more on mortise-and-tenon joints. If affixing panels with rabbets, assemble and glue the frame; wait until it's dry to cut the rabbets. To shape the inside edges, dry-clamp the frame; use a router with a decorative bit.

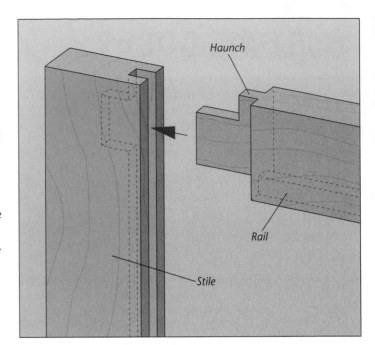

Cutting the panel

TOOLKIT
For flat panel:
• Saw
For raised-bevel panel:
• Clamps
• Table saw, radial-arm saw, or router table with panel-raising bit
For square-shouldered panel:
• Table saw

Making a flat panel

This type of panel is easy to make from 1/4" plywood; there won't be any problem with wood movement. Cut the panel to fit the space, adding on the width of the rabbets or grooves that it will fit into. If it will be placed into a rabbeted frame, make it the exact size; if it will be let into grooves, add 1/16" clearance all around for ease of assembly.

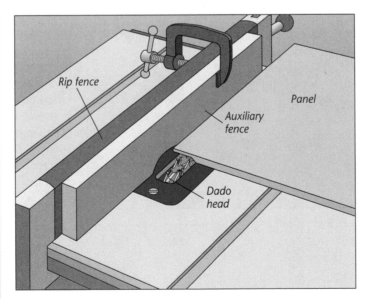

Making a square-shouldered panel

Proceed the same way as for a rabbet cut on the table saw with a standard blade *(page 53)*. Make the cuts on the face first, then make the edge cuts with the panel held vertically. For the vertical cuts, keep the shouldered side of the panel facing out to prevent the waste from binding between the blade and the rip fence.

Making a raised-bevel panel

Use 1/2" to 3/4" solid stock (plywood doesn't bevel well). Make panels up to about 8" wide from a single piece of wood; for wider panels, edge-glue narrower pieces *(page 51)*. Before you cut the panel, with the frame dry-assembled, measure the bottom-to-bottom distance between the grooves. Cut the panel 3/16" to 1/4" short on each side to let the panel "float" in case of wood movement.

A table saw is the first choice for cutting raised bevels, but you could also use a router. In the illustration at left, a dado head is used to cut the bevel. An auxiliary fence is attached to the rip fence to provide sufficient space for the dado head. Tilt the dado about 10° away from the fence, and make test cuts until the cut piece fits into the groove. Make the bevel cuts on all four panel faces. Test the panel for fit; if necessary, adjust the dado and repeat the cuts.

Assembling a grooved frame-and-panel door

TOOLKIT
- Bar or pipe clamps
- Sander

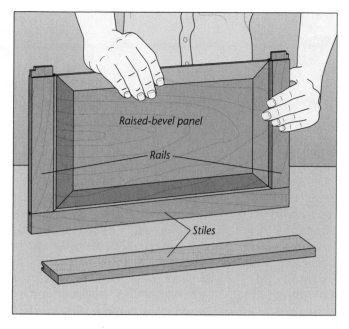

Raised-bevel panel

Rails

Stiles

Joining the rails, stiles, and panel

To assemble your door, you'll need two bar or pipe clamps—one centered under each rail. Be sure the clamps lie on a flat surface; if they're not flat in relation to each other, the door will be twisted. First, apply glue and join one stile and one rail, using dowels or other reinforcement if the joint calls for it; the blind mortise-and-tenon shown at left does not require reinforcement. Slide the panel into the grooves of these two pieces; don't apply any glue to the panel. (Note: To avoid gluing the corners of the panel to the frame, you can round them off slightly and coat the edges with paste wax before inserting it.) Attach the other rail (*left*), and then the second stile. Finally, clamp the assembly securely.

Assembling a rabbeted frame-and-panel door

TOOLKIT
- Router and rabbeting bit
- Clamps (optional)

Cutting the rabbet and installing the panel

To attach a flat plywood panel to rabbets, once the glue on the frame pieces is dry, cut 3/8"x3/8" rabbets on the back of the frame with a router and rabbeting bit. Apply glue sparingly, and evenly, to the rabbets. Press the panel in place, and secure it with clamps, or hammer in brads.

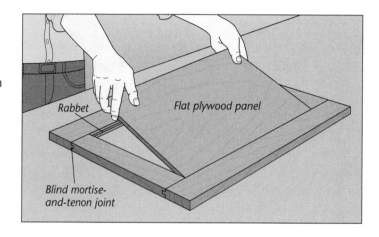

Rabbet

Flat plywood panel

Blind mortise-and-tenon joint

HANGING A DOOR

Door hinges are available in a wide variety of styles, sizes, and finishes to fit flush, lipped, and overlay doors; see page 27 for a look at the hinge styles you might consider. Remember that hardware can determine the type and style of door you will build and use. Don't make hardware an afterthought.

Before hanging a door, be sure the carcase is upright, plumb, and level. If you're installing flush doors, plane them to fit the opening. Your hinge set-up will require careful positioning and cutting of any mortises or other recesses. To hang the door, follow the sequence of steps listed at right; drill body and pilot holes for the screws first (*page 48*), although, with power tools, you might not need to worry about pre-drilling.

Keep in mind these simple tricks: When hanging a lipped door, set the side to be hinged on two pieces of folded sandpaper—one at each end—to raise the door enough to prevent binding. Half the door thick-ness should project beyond the cabinet front or face-frame. For overlay doors, which overlap the door opening edges, fashion a spacer strip to hold the doors at the correct height while you install them.

HANGING BOOKSHELF AND CABINET DOORS

To hang a door on a piece of furniture, proceed as follows:
1. Fasten the hinges on the door.
2. Line up the door and mark the upper screw holes on the carcase or faceframe.
3. Install one upper screw first to ensure alignment; adjust if out of alignment and install other screws.
4. If the swing and alignment are all right, install a bottom screw and recheck the swing; adjust if necessary and install remaining screws.

SHELVING

Without shelves, cabinets and bookcases would just be simple cases that offer no place to store, display, or hold your belongings. But as well as being functional, shelves serve an aesthetic purpose. Deciding on how and where to place the shelves makes each unit different. You might use fixed shelves, adjustable shelves, or a combination of the two. Balance sturdiness with economy, aesthetics, and convenience.

Although there are many ways to make a solid unit, fixed shelves—dadoed into the sides—strengthen the case. Make sure at least the bottom and top shelves are both fixed in place; if the case is over 4 feet tall, fasten at least one middle shelf as well. Keep in mind that fixed shelves, though rigid and good-looking, are hard to change if you want to redesign the unit.

Adjustable shelves offer a lot more flexibility; support them with tracks and clips, or with pegs *(page 29)*. You can even raise the bottom shelf off the floor to allow room for a kickspace. Surface mount the tracks, or recess them into grooves. With pegs, choose between short lengths of 1/4-inch-diameter hardwood dowel and a variety of manufactured styles *(page 29)*. Whichever type of peg you choose, you'll need two rows of 1/4-inch holes in each side piece or partition.

Dimensions: Your only restriction is shelf span: Bookshelves longer than 24 inches sag if made from 3/4-inch particleboard. Better grades of fir or pine span 32 inches; 3/4-inch plywood and most hardwoods stay relatively straight at 36 to 40 inches in length. Support longer shelves along the back with cleats, or use partitions.

Materials: Use plywood for large units; it's easy to work, cheap, and strong. Solid lumber is also good; No. 2 Common pine is economical. For hardwoods, use 1-by stock.

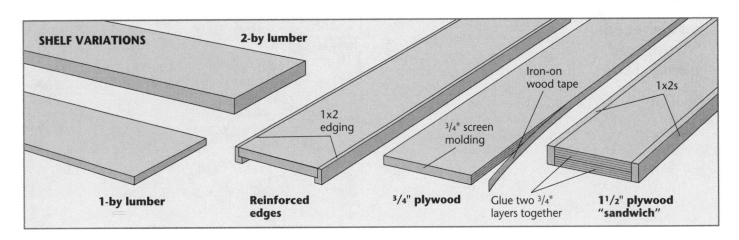

SHELF VARIATIONS

2-by lumber

1-by lumber

Reinforced edges

1x2 edging

3/4" screen molding

Iron-on wood tape

Glue two 3/4" layers together

3/4" plywood

1x2s

1 1/2" plywood "sandwich"

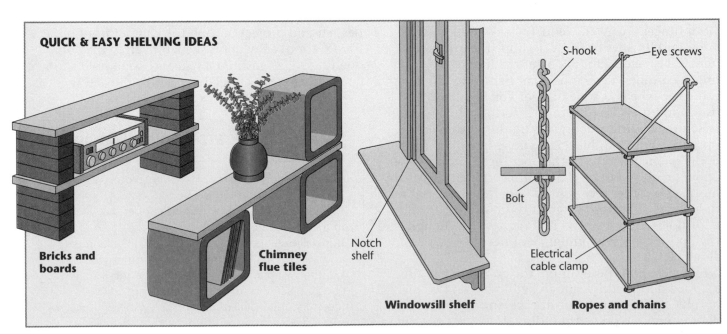

QUICK & EASY SHELVING IDEAS

Bricks and boards

Chimney flue tiles

Notch shelf

Windowsill shelf

S-hook

Eye screws

Bolt

Electrical cable clamp

Ropes and chains

INSTALLING SHELVES

I t's vital to cut and join pieces carefully when installing shelves. To attach a fixed shelf to the inner sides of a bookcase or cabinet, use a dado joint *(page 54)*; for a more finished effect, stop the dado 1/2 inch from the front edge. To join the top to the sides, choose from the options shown below. For more on cutting these joints, see page 52. If you don't want fasteners to be visible on the outside of your case, when using butt joints, reinforce them with biscuits *(page 64)*; no plugs or putty will mar the outside surface.

For adjustable shelves, decide beforehand on either back- or side-mounting. See page 78 for details.

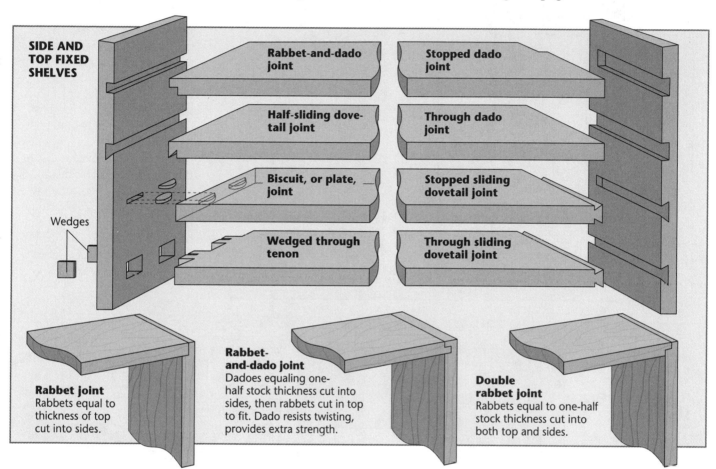

SIDE AND TOP FIXED SHELVES

Rabbet-and-dado joint

Stopped dado joint

Half-sliding dovetail joint

Through dado joint

Biscuit, or plate, joint

Stopped sliding dovetail joint

Wedges

Wedged through tenon

Through sliding dovetail joint

Rabbet joint
Rabbets equal to thickness of top cut into sides.

Rabbet-and-dado joint
Dadoes equaling one-half stock thickness cut into sides, then rabbets cut in top to fit. Dado resists twisting, provides extra strength.

Double rabbet joint
Rabbets equal to one-half stock thickness cut into both top and sides.

Securing fixed shelving

TOOLKIT
- Circular saw
- Square
- Sander or sandpaper
- Clamps
- Router with appropriate bits
- Drill and bit for peg-type supports
- Screwdriver (optional)
- Screws, nails, glue
- Hammer or mallet

1 ▶ **Dry-fitting and glue-up**
Once you've cut your shelves and prepared the sides of the unit, dry-fit the assembly and make any adjustments. For shelf dadoes and rabbet-type joints, use fasteners and glue.

To glue up the assembly, lay one side piece face down on a flat surface. Spread glue evenly in all dadoes and rabbets; coat the end grain of the matching pieces. Put the bottom shelf into its dado and tap it home with a beating block and hammer. Once all the fixed shelves are upright in their dadoes, quickly add the other side piece before the glue dries. If you have a few shelves, put them in using only hand pressure, then tap them in place *(right)*.

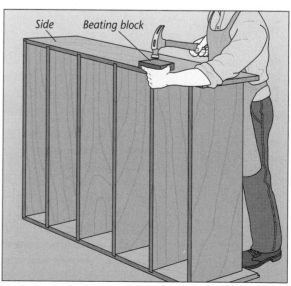

Side   Beating block

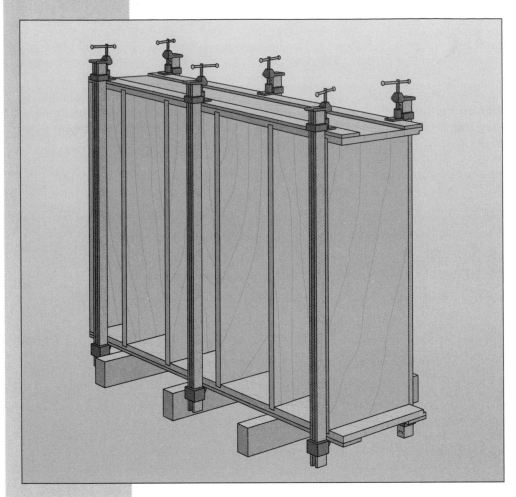

2 Fastening and clamping

To tighten up the shelves in the dadoes, use pipe or bar clamps—unless you're fastening them with screws. Starting with the bottom shelf, place one clamp across the front of the case and another across the back, aligning them over the dadoes as shown at left. (Positioning the clamp—and adding wood scraps to protect the sides—can be maddening; get a helper.) Slowly tighten the clamps, alternating between them. Stop when you feel the shelf bottom out in the dado, or when you see glue squeeze out. If you're using nails, drive one in the center of each side between the two clamps. Then remove one of the clamps and, on each side, drive a nail in its place. Repeat for the other clamp. If you're relying on glue alone, clamp the front and back of each shelf, square the case, and leave the clamps overnight.

Securing adjustable shelving

TOOLKIT
- Measuring tape
- Screwdriver
- Pencil or chalk
- Drill with appropriate bits
- Commercial or homemade jig
- Stop collar
- Carpenter's level
- Hammer or mallet
- Sleeve-setting punch
- Router with rabbeting bit (optional)

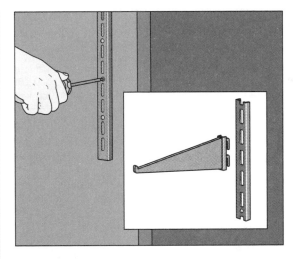

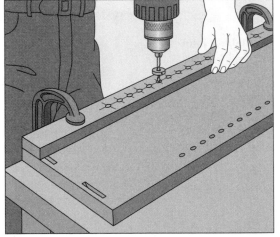

Preparing for back-mounted and side-mounted shelving

To install typical back-mounted shelving, attach tracks 16 to 32 inches apart, depending on design and load. Fasten one track into the back of the case using screws. Drive the first screw loosely (above, left), plumb the track, then install the second track exactly level with the first one. Once the tracks are in place, hang the brackets (inset) at the desired height by inserting their ends into the slots.

For side shelf supports, drill two parallel rows of holes in the side panels. Use a commercial jig for perfectly aligned holes, or make your own jig from 1x3 stock (above, right). Use a bit the same diameter as the sleeves—either commercial hardware or dowel pegs—with a stop collar to mark drilling depth. For more on shelf support options, turn to page 29.

FINISHING

Furniture lasts longer when it has received a fine finish. This will protect the piece from dirt, abrasion, moisture, heat, and chemicals. You can choose to coat your projects with two basic types of finishes: those that penetrate wood pores and those that you build up in layers on top of the surface. The chart on page 31 will help you decide on the best choice for your particular project.

A good finish depends on proper preparation. Before you can apply any finish you must repair any surface flaws or irregularities by finish-sanding and removing any raised wood fibers. Then fill and sand as required. Turn to the section beginning on page 80 for more on the steps involved. Once the surface is as good as you can make it, you're ready for the finish itself. Whatever your choice—from oil finishes and shellacs to lacquers and varnishes—test the finish first on a piece of scrap wood left over from your project to make sure you'll be getting the result you want. Once it is applied you may choose to finish the finish—rubbing or waxing what you have applied to create a custom sheen. You'll find more information on the proper techniques on page 88.

There are a variety of ways to apply a finish, including brushing, wiping, and spraying. This chapter will show you how to master these different techniques.

PREPARING THE SURFACE

Surface preparation may not be an immediately rewarding task, but it is essential to ensure that your cabinet or bookcase ends up with a finish that is beautiful and long lasting.

Making wood repairs: Sand out surface imperfections such as scratches; plane any remaining mill marks. Fill more severe lumber defects *(page 19)* with patching material *(below)*. Keep in mind that patched areas can look lighter or darker than the rest of the piece after you have applied a stain or clear finish. Test on a scrap piece first.

Finish-sanding and grain-raising: Use progressively finer grits each time you sand. You may want to raise the grain, particularly if using a water-base finish. Both these procedures are discussed opposite.

Filling and sealing: Cutting open-grain woods such as oak, ash, and walnut exposes large pores that need to be filled before applying shellac, lacquer, or varnish to ensure a fine finish. If you use a sealer, apply it just before the top coat. You can also use a sealer before you stain *(page 81)*.

Filling surface flaws

TOOLKIT
- Putty knife
- Sander (for large holes)

OR
- Soldering gun or other smokeless heat source

Using wood patching compound
Choose a compound that is compatible with the ingredients and color of finish you have selected. Apply the material by flexing a putty knife blade to drive in the patching compound *(right)*. On large voids, use a few thin applications; leave the last layer higher than the surface and sand later.

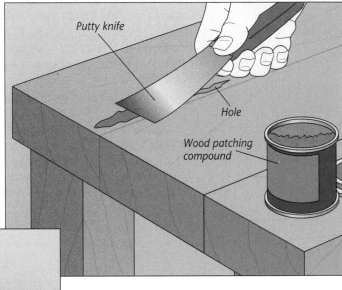

Putty knife

Hole

Wood patching compound

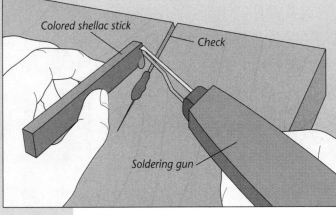

Colored shellac stick

Check

Soldering gun

Using a shellac stick
Often used for furniture repairs, shellac sticks—sometimes called burn-in sticks—also work well for a range of surface imperfections on new wood, including small checks, dings, joint lines, and scratches. You can buy sticks that are clear, or in a range of wood tones; choose the color closest to your finish, since shellac absorbs little stain. Press the tip of a soldering gun on the shellac stick to heat it, melting the shellac into the flaw *(left)*.

Finish-sanding

TOOLKIT
- Sander
- Vacuum cleaner (if you will be using a water-base finish)

Sanding with fine-grit paper
To spot-sand patching materials, small gouges, or scratches, return briefly to a coarser grit. Sand only with the grain, and sand end grain in one direction only. Reach into corners and crevices using a hand scraper, emery board, or the crisp, folded edge of a new sheet of sandpaper. As you progress with finer grits of paper, check your work with a low-angle light. Each finer grit should remove scratches made by the previous grit. Then vacuum the entire piece to pick up fine dust particles. For finishes other than water-base ones, you can wipe the surface with a tack cloth, which you can make by wetting cheesecloth with mineral spirits and varnish.

Raising the grain

Swelling and smoothing the wood fibers

If you'll be using a water-base stain or finish, you should raise the wood's grain and remove the raised fibers; with other types of finishes, you won't need to do this unless the wood has a naturally fuzzy surface. To raise the grain, swell the wood fibers by wiping the surface with a damp sponge *(right)*; let the wood dry. Then sand the fibers down with a fine-grit sandpaper. Repeat the process once or twice.

Damp sponge
Swollen wood fibers

Filling the grain

Applying wood filler

Paste fillers are the most common; silicate formulas do the best job. They are neutral-colored and typically have the consistency of peanut butter. Thin the filler according to label instructions and color it with stain pigments. Or buy premixed filler, available in a number of shades. If you'll be using light-colored stain, apply the filler first. For darker stains, make your filler at least one shade darker than the stain and use it after staining. Apply the filler with burlap or a soft cloth, using a circular motion to work it into the pores. Do a final light wipe with the grain, then allow the filler to dry for 24 hours. For sanding, follow the label instructions for the product you're using.

Sealing wood

Applying a sealer

A sealer, sanded after it dries, forms a solid bond between wood and the top coat, sealing off stain and filler so the finish won't get cloudy. The best sealer is often a wash coat—a thinned-down coat of your final finish—compatibility won't be an issue. If finishing with shellac or lacquer, try 1 pound of shellac flakes dissolved in 1 gallon of denatured alcohol—a "1-pound cut"— as a sealer after filler and stain coats. You can also buy quick-drying sealers and sanding sealers; follow application and sanding instructions. Sealers can also be used at earlier stages. On softwoods, a coat under the stain gives more even penetration, eliminating the mottled look of stained pine or the high-contrast stripes of darkly stained fir plywood. Seal end grain before applying stain, since these areas tend to drink up stain at a faster rate. Because sealers absorb stains differently, always try out your stain and sealer on a test patch. Remove all sanding residue.

ASK A PRO

STEAMING OUT A DENT

You can repair most dents in wood by steaming them out. Simply cover the crushed wood fibers with a damp towel and hold a hot steam iron on the towel until it begins to dry out (right). Check your wood, then remoisten the towel and repeat the procedure several times, as needed.

Damp towel

STAINING

Many woods—cherry, walnut, and mahogany, for example—have a beautiful natural color that requires no stain at all. But on light-colored, nondescript woods, stain adds some color and a bit of character. It can also highlight the grain figure and in some cases enable a nondescript wood to take on the appearance of a more desirable species. Ebony, for example, is an extremely expensive wood, only available in small pieces. But an often-used staining technique known as ebonizing can turn more commonly available woods like maple, holly, and birch into a reasonable facsimile of ebony. Stains have been used throughout woodworking history to make light woods dark, common woods fancy, and streaked woods more uniform.

Wood stains fall into two general categories: pigments and dyes. Pigmented stains are composed of finely ground particles of color held in suspension in oil, resins, or solvent. Essentially a thin, opaque paint, this type of stain coats the wood fibers and tends to conceal the grain. Most wood dyes are aniline (a coal-tar derivative) dyes, which are dissolved in a number of media. These dyes are actually absorbed by the wood fibers, allowing the grain to show through. The pigments in stains create a more superficial color. Once the solvent evaporates, the pigments remain on the surface.

The tendency toward "one-step" products in recent years has led to stain/filler combinations, pigmented sealers, and all-in-one stain finishes. Many of these products work well, although you have less control over each step of the process. See the chart on page 31 for more information on the characteristics of some categories of stains.

Applying pigmented oil stains

TOOLKIT
• Natural-bristle paintbrush (optional)

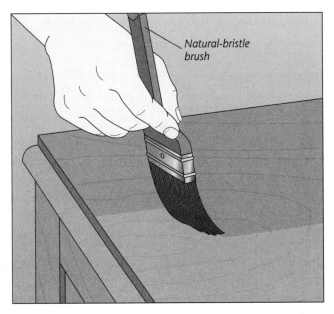

Natural-bristle brush

1 Brushing on the stain
These popular, ready-mixed stains, sold as oil stain, wood stain, and pigmented wiping stain, are nonfading, nonbleeding, and easy to apply. However, you should not use them on unfilled open-grain woods such as oak; their heavy pigments fill up surface pores but do not penetrate the hard grain. Keep in mind, too, that cracks, dents, or scratches in the wood will catch more than their share of the pigments and will stand out when the finish is applied. Stir these stains well before and during use. Brush the stain into the wood *(left)*, or wipe it on with a lint-free cloth using small, circular motions.

2 Removing the excess
Wipe off the excess stain immediately with a clean cloth, as shown at right. When the cloth is soaked, dispose of it to avoid any fire or ventilation hazards. Wait 12 to 24 hours before proceeding to the next step—sealing the wood.

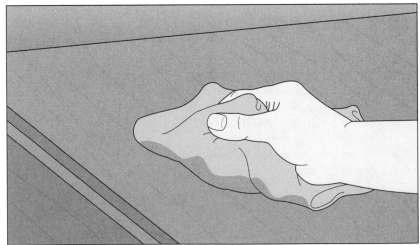

Applying penetrating oil stains

Wiping on the stain
Though often confused with pigmented stains, these are actually dyes carried by an oil/resin medium. Commonly known as colored Danish oil, or colored penetrating oil, these stains are popular because they provide color and finish in the same coat, while allowing the wood grain to show through. Apply penetrating oil stains with a clean, lint-free cloth, then use the same cloth to remove any excess oil and to equalize the surface color as much as possible. Wipe the stain while it's still wet, making the last strokes parallel to the grain.

Applying water-base aniline dyes

TOOLKIT
• Synthetic-bristle paintbrush or spray gun

Brushing or spraying on the dye
Generally sold in powdered form and mixed with hot water, these stains are clear, permanent, and brilliant in color. They contain no flammable solvents, have no odor, and clean up easily. However, water stains swell the wood fibers, so you'll have to raise the grain first (page 81). These stains also take at least 24 hours to dry. Water-base stains are effective on woods such as oak, cherry, and walnut—woods that require only a slight boost in color to bring out their natural vibrancy. Always keep in mind, however, that the stain will appear slightly darker in solution than after it has dried on the wood. Using water-base aniline dye is as simple as applying it with a paintbrush, or spraying it on (page 86). Be careful not to flood the surface of the work or you may end up loosening glue joints and extending the drying time.

Applying alcohol-base aniline dyes

TOOLKIT
• Spray gun

Spraying on the dye
Using a spray gun (page 86) is the best way to apply alcohol-base aniline dyes (sometimes called spirit-soluble stains); use the type of sprayer powered by an air compressor. These dyes don't raise the grain, but on the other hand, they aren't very light-fast. They do, however, yield hues that are brighter and more lively than do other categories of stains. Alcohol-base aniline dyes are very quick-drying, and this is why it is best to spray them onto the work surface. If you attempt to apply them in any other manner, you may be forced to deal with unsightly lap marks showing through your finish.

Applying non-grain-raising stains

TOOLKIT
• Spray gun
OR
• Retarder
• Synthetic-bristle paintbrush

Brushing or spraying on the stain
A favorite of the furniture and cabinet making industries, non-grain-raising (NGR) stains are available only in a premixed liquid form—this makes them more convenient to use, as there is no fussing with measuring and mixing solvents and solute, and no extra mess to clean up afterward. Combining the best qualities of water and alcohol-base stains with none of their disadvantages, these stains are light-fast and—as their name implies—won't raise the grain. NGR stains are not recommended for softwoods because they penetrate the wood fibers unevenly, leaving an imperfect finish. Because they dry so quickly, it is advised that NGR stains are sprayed onto the wood—wear a respirator and watch out for open flames or sparks. You can also add a retarder so that the drying time limit is extended a little—this affords you the opportunity to brush on the stain more easily.

APPLYING OIL FINISHES

The first wood finish was most likely oil-based, and this category of finish is still very popular. But many of today's so-called oil products contain polymers, resins, and driers, giving them some of the superior properties of varnish and other harder, more durable finishes.

Penetrating resins: These products—Danish oil, teak oil, antique oil, or penetrating oil sealer—are simple to apply, and are thus very popular. They preserve the wood's feel and produce a relatively durable finish that can easily be renewed. They are best for hard, open-grain woods such as oak, producing mixed results on softwoods and closed-grain hardwoods, and darkening the surface of some woods objectionably. Test the product on scrap first.

Mineral oil: This clear, viscous, nontoxic oil is a good choice for wooden bowls, eating utensils, and cutting boards. But don't expect much more than a warm glow and a slight renewing of the surface.

Tung oil: This natural oil, built up in thin coats, produces a relatively hard finish that resists abrasion, water, heat, and acid. Its sheen increases with each coat, but it will never develop a high gloss. A true tung oil finish should be either 100 percent tung oil or polymerized tung oil. The latter has polymer resins and driers added for a faster-drying hard finish with a higher sheen.

Boiled linseed oil: Old-timers may swear by this finish, but the hours or even days it takes each coat to dry, and the number of coats required, make it impractical for most projects. In addition, it's a rather soft finish that doesn't take kindly to water, heat, or chemicals.

On this page you'll find easy-to-follow instructions for applying some of these oil finishes.

Applying penetrating resin

1 ▶ Applying the flood coat
Stain the wood first (*page 82*), or use a tinted penetrating resin. Don't use a filler or sealer. Pour a generous amount of resin for the first coat (the flood coat) and spread it around the surface with a rag *(right)*. Let it dry for 15 to 30 minutes, then wipe it off with a soft cloth, following the direction of the wood grain. Apply more coats to build up the finish, as desired. Consult manufacturer's directions for drying time.

Penetrating resin

Rag

Flood coat

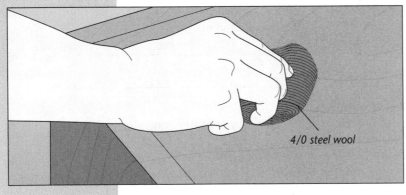

4/0 steel wool

◀ 2 Increasing the sheen
If you want greater luster, once the surface is completely dry, rub briskly in the direction of the grain with 4/0 steel wool and a little resin. Wipe the surface clean, let it dry overnight, and follow up by applying two or more coats of paste wax, as described on page 88.

Applying tung oil

Rubbing in the oil
You'll need a soft, lint-free cloth and a lamb's wool buffer. Thin 100% tung oil with mineral spirits—thick coats may wrinkle, hiding the wood below.

Rub the oil into the wood with the cloth. Apply at least two coats, letting each dry as long as the product label recommends, then buff the surface.

APPLYING SHELLAC

Shellac provides a warm and subtle look and feel to a finished project. Buy shellac in either dry or premixed liquid form. The orange type is standard; white shellac has been bleached so it won't impart an amber tone to the wood, but it's significantly less moisture-resistant and has a much shorter shelf life than the orange type.

Shellac is vulnerable to a spilled cocktail, strong soaps and detergents, and even water. Also, if exposed to much moisture, it turns cloudy.

Thinned with alcohol, successive coats of shellac dry and bond quickly. You must build up the surface with several coats before the finish takes on a luster.

BUYING AND MIXING SHELLAC

Shellac deteriorates with age. Always buy it in small quantities from a dealer with enough turnover to ensure that the stock is fresh. When in doubt as to the shellac's age, test it on scrap. If it takes a long time to dry or remains tacky, don't use it.

You can buy flake (dry) shellac by the pound. The amount you add to a gallon of alcohol determines the strength of the solution, measured in "cuts." For a 1-pound cut, dissolve 1 pound of flakes in 1 gallon of denatured alcohol; a 2-pound cut requires 2 pounds of flakes to a gallon, and so on. If you've never worked with shellac before, begin with a 1-pound cut. Once you have some experience, move to a 2- or 3-pound cut.

You can buy liquid (dissolved) shellac in 3- or 4-pound cuts. To make a 1-pound cut from a 4-pound one, add 3 parts alcohol to 1 part dissolved shellac.

Applying shellac

TOOLKIT
- Natural-bristle brush
- Sander (optional)

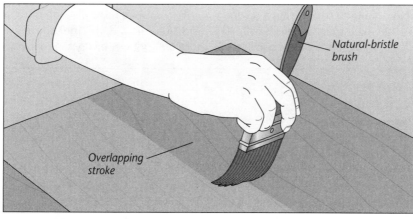

Natural-bristle brush

Overlapping stroke

1 Brushing on shellac
Begin by brushing on a full coat of shellac, using a slow, smooth motion. Take special care to overlap all adjoining brushstrokes *(left)*. This will help keep ridges and streaks to a minimum.

2 Sanding the surface
After about an hour, sand or rub off ridges and brushstrokes with 320-grit sandpaper *(left)* or 4/0 steel wool (in line with wood grain). The shellac should sand to a powder; if it clogs the paper, wait a few more minutes before continuing.

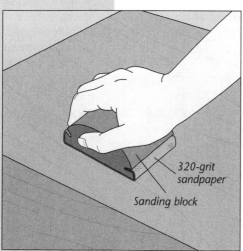

320-grit sandpaper

Sanding block

3 Building up the finish
Apply a second coat the same way as the first, then sand or rub it down after 1 hour of drying. The third coat should be smooth enough for final rubbing; if not, sand one last time and apply more shellac. Continue until you build up the finish you desire. Then use 4/0 steel wool and lubricating oil *(page 88)* to dull the surface gloss. For a classic high-gloss look, allow at least 3 days for the finish to harden, then polish with pumice, rottenstone, or 600-grit wet-or-dry sandpaper. Follow with wax.

APPLYING LACQUER

Spraying on clear lacquer is an efficient process—it dries within seconds, eliminating any dust problems, and you can apply many coats quickly. It's not as moisture-proof as varnish, but it is very durable and you can rub it to a high gloss. Lacquer layers as easily as shellac, yet it's more heat- and chemical-resistant. It won't fill pores in open-grain wood; use filler and sealer.

The lacquer available today is basically nitrocellulose modified with oils and resins, then dissolved in solvents.

Spraying and brushing lacquer are basically the same, and will produce essentially the same finish, but brushing lacquer evaporates more slowly, giving brush marks time to level out. Both types are available in flat, semigloss, and gloss finishes. Never apply spraying lacquer with a brush, or vice versa. For best results, thin lacquer according to the label instructions. If you've used pigmented oil stain, use a wash coat of shellac or sanding sealer to reduce the risk of incompatibility.

Brushing on lacquer

TOOLKIT
• Wide natural-bristle brush
• Sander

Natural-bristle brush

1 Applying the first coat
Begin by brushing the lacquer onto the wood in a smooth coat. Working rapidly with a wide brush to speed things along, spread the lacquer with long strokes without too much back-and-forth brushing, and with little overlap between adjacent strokes (*left*). Keep your working area small and finish one area at a time.

2 Applying additional coats
Even though your surface will dry dust-free in minutes, wait at least 1 hour before sanding or applying a second coat. Then carefully level any high spots or defects with 400-grit sandpaper. Apply additional coats until you build up the desired finish; two coats over a sealer is a bare minimum. If you want a relatively high gloss, after the final coat has dried overnight, rub the surface with rottenstone, pumice, or 600-grit wet-or-dry sandpaper (*page 88*).

Spraying on lacquer

TOOLKIT
• Air compressor and spray gun
OR
• Lacquer in aerosol can

Using a spray gun
If possible, use a well-ventilated spray booth to keep dust away and to prevent overspray from spreading beyond your work area. Wear a respirator, and watch out for open flame or sparks in the area. Follow the manufacturer's instructions to set up the spray gun, and thin the lacquer according to label directions. Holding the gun 8" to 10" away from the work surface, spray from side to side, making overlapping passes (*below, left*).

Let it dry, then apply each successive coat in a pattern perpendicular to the previous one until you have built up the finish to your satisfaction. If you choose to use lacquer in an aerosol spray can as shown (*below, right*), hold the can 10" to 12" from the work while spraying. This method produces good results for small surfaces, but requires many coats, since the lacquer is highly thinned in order to flow through the can's spray nozzle.

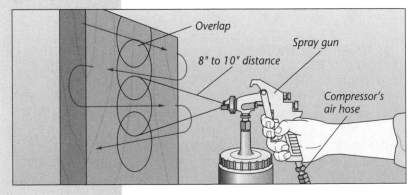

Overlap
Spray gun
8" to 10" distance
Compressor's air hose

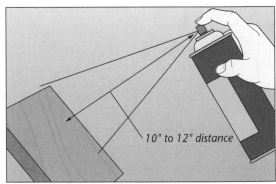

10" to 12" distance

APPLYING VARNISH

A varnish finish ensures that your project will be durable, moisture- and heat-resistant, and attractive. You can buy varnish in either the gloss or semi-gloss (sometimes called matte or satin) sheen. Some of the different types of varnishes are described below—all vary in their characteristics.

Polyurethane varnish: This tough finish is the ultimate in resistance to abrasion, moisture, heat, and chemicals, though it can be somewhat brittle. It's suited for high-use areas such as tabletops. Keep in mind that once polyurethane has cured, you can't remove it with solvents, and new coats won't chemically bond to it.

If the surface is prepared by sanding (to provide a mechanical bond), polyurethane can be used over almost any finish unless there is a chemical reaction. To ensure an additional coat will bond to the first, make sure the first coat isn't completely cured.

Alkyd varnish: Traditionally used for furniture and often referred to as oil-base varnish, this type is not as hard as polyurethane, but it's more flexible; you can recoat without worrying about bonding. A tung-oil base makes it particularly moisture-resistant. Like most varnishes, it can darken over time, but you can remove it with paint stripper.

Water-base varnishes: Nontoxic and easy to clean up, these "latex" acrylic varnishes perform reasonably well, but lack the chemical resistance of polyurethane and the heat and moisture resistance of other varnishes.

Because water-base varnishes are about 70 percent water, it takes several coats to achieve the same buildup as one coat of alkyd varnish. The water content will also raise the grain, which you can deal with by either sanding off after the first coat has dried or raising it intentionally beforehand *(page 81)*.

Rub-on varnish: To apply this penetrating resin and varnish mixture, rub it on like a penetrating resin finish *(page 84)*. Because of its higher solids content, it builds up in layers on the surface. Each application increases the sheen, but there's a trade-off with the durability of rub-on varnish and its ease of application. Like other penetrating finishes, it darkens wood; also, it's irreversible on open-grain woods.

To apply varnish, you simply need to brush it on. See the step-by-step instructions below.

Applying varnish

TOOLKIT
- Vacuum cleaner
- Paintbrush (natural-bristle for oil-base varnishes; synthetic paintbrush or foam brush for water-base)

1 Preparing the workpiece
Woodworkers rarely use fillers with varnishes, but a sealer is always a good idea. Use a thinned-down solution of the varnish as a sealer. Since varnish remains tacky for 2 to 6 hours, dust is its main enemy. Pick a clean workspace and vacuum all surfaces a few hours before setting up. Make sure the room is warm enough—this can make a big difference in drying time.

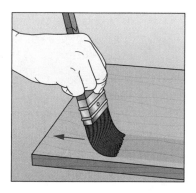  

2 Brushing on varnish
Apply varnish sparingly. Test on a piece of scrap wood first. If air bubbles remain in the cured finish, thin the varnish with about 15% mineral spirits. Apply evenly with long, smooth strokes parallel to the grain *(above, left)*, quickly brush across the grain *(above, center)*, then "tip off" along the grain, using only the very tips of the bristles *(above, right)*. Use the least number of brushstrokes you can, and work in one small section at a time. Finish the piece section by section without creating lap marks. To detect dry spots, direct an angled light on the work. For additional coats, remove the gloss with 400-grit sandpaper. Build up the surface with gloss varnish, then use abrasives to achieve the final sheen. Once dry, rub lightly with 4/0 steel wool for a satin finish, or with pumice, rottenstone, or 600-grit wet-or-dry paper for a high gloss *(page 88)*.

FINISHING THE FINISH

To give your project a final touch of elegance, simply rub or wax the top coat of your finish. Rubbing removes lint, dust, and brush marks so the surfaces reflect light uniformly, increasing the sheen. Waxing adds depth and luster, and protects the finish.

Rubbing: Use both a lubricant, traditionally paraffin oil, but almost any kind of oil, or even water, will do, and an abrasive. Mineral spirits and wet-or-dry sand-

paper are also options; try 400, 500, then 600 grits wrapped around a sanding block. If you like a less matte finish, buff with a lamb's wool pad; for extra gloss, try commercial products for power buffers.

Waxing: Inexpensive and easy to use, make your own traditional wax by dissolving beeswax in turpentine. You can also buy paste wax, which contains carnauba wax, creating a more durable finish.

Rubbing a finish

TOOLKIT
• Cork sanding pad or blackboard eraser

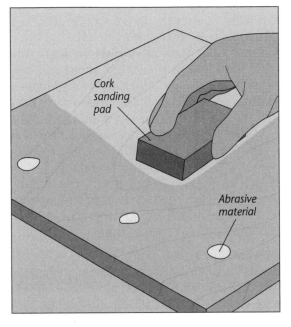

Cork sanding pad

Abrasive material

Applying the abrasive and rubbing
Spread lubricant (paraffin oil, mineral oil, or water) in a thin film over the surface. For a matte finish, rub with FFF-grade ground pumice. Shake it on sparingly. For a glossier finish, choose rottenstone. You can use a commercial rubbing compound instead. Rub the abrasives across the lubricated surface, using a cork sanding pad *(left)* or a blackboard eraser. Keep strokes long and even, and rub in the direction of the grain. Once you've rubbed the entire surface, wipe off the slurry that's formed and check for any spots that still gleam. Keep rubbing until they're gone. Complete the job by wiping off all the oil with a soft cloth.

Waxing a finish

TOOLKIT
• Power buffer (optional)

Applying wax
Spoon the wax onto a moist cloth (old socks are useful), then fold the cloth around the wax to make an "applicator." Rub the wax into the finish, using large, circular motions *(right)*. Apply just enough to create a thin film; excess wax will dull the surface and make it gummy. Let the wax dry for a few minutes (or for the time indicated on the label), then buff the surface with a soft cloth or with a power buffer fitted with a pad made of felt or lamb's wool.

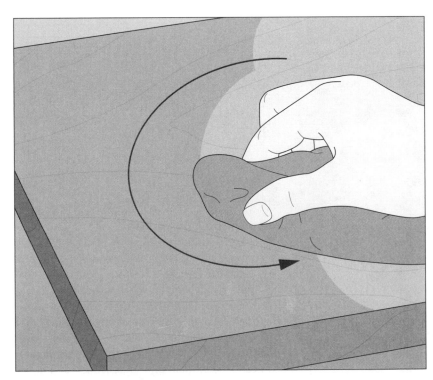

PROJECTS

After reading about the proper construction and finishing techniques—and the tools necessary to achieve satisfying results—it's time to put your talents to the test. This section offers a host of simple and practical bookshelf and cabinet projects from which to choose.

Whether it's a simple backless bookcase for your study *(page 92),* an easy-to-build bookcase to go in your child's bedroom *(page 93),* or a corner cabinet for your dining room *(page 96),* the units featured should offer something to fit your needs and taste.

Keep in mind, however, that although a certain amount of detail is provided with each unit, it will not take you through each step of the project as full-blown plans do; in some cases, a particular joinery method or detailed measurements are highlighted. Also, depending on the project and how it will fit with its surrounding decor, you might want to choose one building material over another, melamine for plywood or plywood for solid wood, for example.

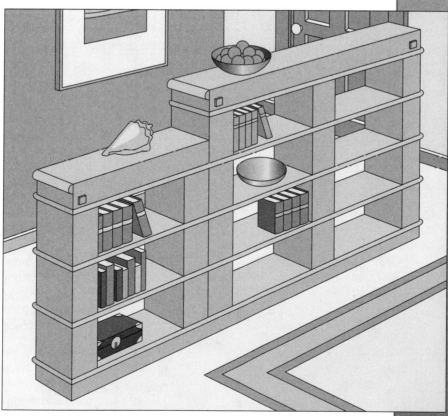

This freestanding combination bookcase and room divider helps define different areas of a room while offering display and storage space. To see how it's put together, turn to page 94.

PLYWOOD ETAGERE

The carcase and shelves of this cute étagère are made from ³/₄-inch plywood, with a 1x3 faceframe covering the edges; banding hides the edges of the shelving.

Cut the sides, top, and bottom of the unit to length and then rip them to width. Cut the shelves to size, making the first shelf 1¹/₂ inches wider so it overhangs the doors; notch the front edges of the shelf to accommodate the faceframe. Mark the locations of the shelves and bottom in the side panels and rout dadoes. Rout a ¹/₄-inch by ¹/₄-inch rabbet in the sides and top to accept the back panel. Also cut a ³/₈-inch by ³/₄-inch rabbet in the side panels for the top. Add glue to the dadoes, fit the shelves and bottom in place, then secure with finishing nails. Glue and nail the top in place, then add the decorative molding.

The faceframe is glued and nailed to the carcase. Sketch out the decorative upper part of the faceframe before cutting. Nail a 1-inch by ³/₄-inch rail underneath the lower shelf. Cut the doors to size and mount them with flush hinges (page 27). Add the decorative footing to the unit and tack the molding to the top. Conceal nail holes with wood filler before sanding and painting.

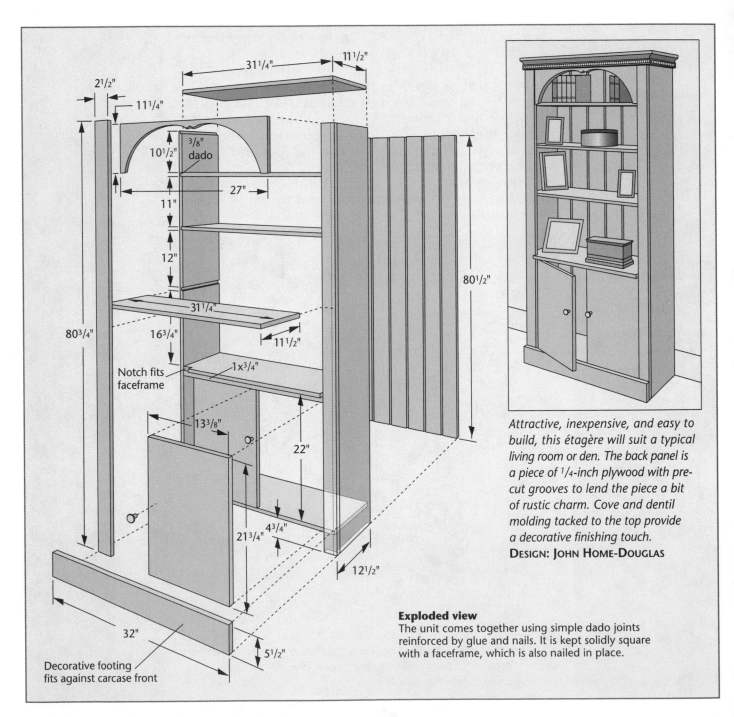

Attractive, inexpensive, and easy to build, this étagère will suit a typical living room or den. The back panel is a piece of ¹/₄-inch plywood with pre-cut grooves to lend the piece a bit of rustic charm. Cove and dentil molding tacked to the top provide a decorative finishing touch.

DESIGN: JOHN HOME-DOUGLAS

Exploded view
The unit comes together using simple dado joints reinforced by glue and nails. It is kept solidly square with a faceframe, which is also nailed in place.

MAGAZINE RACK

Construct this ladder-style unit with 1x3 uprights and shelves cut to size *(right)*. Round off upright tops, then rout out shelf dadoes. Plan for 12-inch-high shelves and seven-inch-high acrylic front strips to fit most magazines—alter measurements as needed. Glue and nail shelves to uprights, then add nail rails.

Sand and finish the unit, then screw the 1/4-inch acrylic pieces in place (don't over-tighten). Fasten the unit to wall studs, or anchor it with toggle bolts.

Keep all your magazines and catalogs together—and in order—with this simple magazine rack. Use an economical softwood grade, then sand and finish it for a professional look.

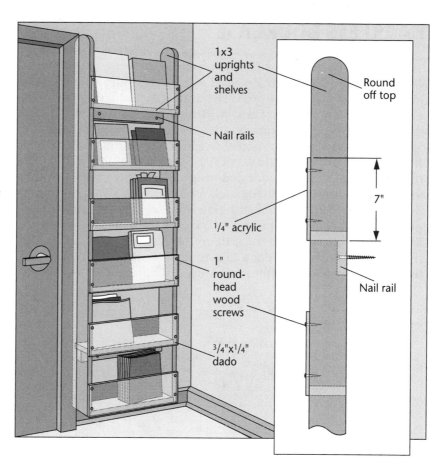

- 1x3 uprights and shelves
- Nail rails
- 1/4" acrylic
- 1" round-head wood screws
- 3/4"x1/4" dado
- Round off top
- 7"
- Nail rail

BOOKCASE MODULE

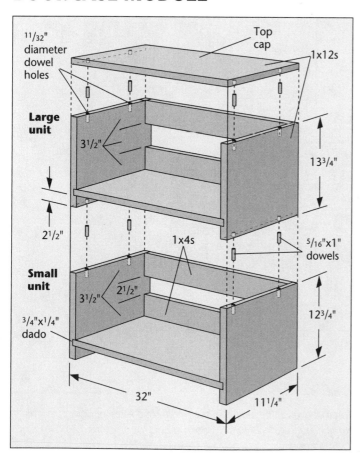

- 11/32" diameter dowel holes
- Top cap
- 1x12s
- **Large unit**
- 3 1/2"
- 13 3/4"
- 2 1/2"
- 1x4s
- 5/16"x1" dowels
- **Small unit**
- 3 1/2"
- 2 1/2"
- 3/4"x1/4" dado
- 12 3/4"
- 32"
- 11 1/4"

To build a module, cut the 1x12 sides and shelf and the 1x4 back slats to length. Allow more height in some units for larger books and photo albums.

Rout shelf dadoes in the side panels. Glue and nail all joints. Glue on the back slats and nail them through the sides. Drill slightly oversized holes for the dowels that hold the unit together *(left)*.

For a finished look, add a top cap. Sand the unit, then finish as desired.

This versatile book-case is actually constructed of three different stacking modules—add or remove the separate units as your needs and tastes change. Each unit can be as small or as large as books and other belongings require.

BACKLESS BOOKCASE

This simple bookcase project is made entirely from standard 1x8 pine. Cut the top and sides to length and join the sides to the top using rabbet joints as shown. The bottom is cut to length and attached to the sides using dado joints. See the inset at right for proper dado depth. The shelves and shelf supports are ripped to width—6 inches in this case—and then cut to length. Attach the shelves to the sides using blind dadoes. Make sure the single shelf in the middle section is staggered—not on the same plane as those on the sides—so that dadoes don't conflict; this also provides room for a tall decorative element such as a plant.

Mitered molding tacked and glued to the sides of the bookcase at the top provides a decorative touch; a 1x2 kickplate nailed through the sides helps fill out the bottom. Sand the unit and, if desired, stain it. Top with a polyurethane satin finish coat. For a different look, attach a plywood or hardboard back painted to match the room's decor.

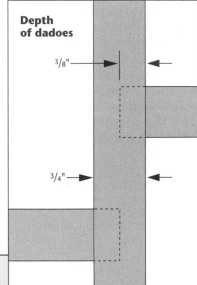

Depth of dadoes

$3/8"$

$3/4"$

Shelves
To support the shelves, cut blind dadoes in the vertical pieces with a $3/4"$ straight router bit. Square the dadoes with a chisel and notch both ends of each shelf.

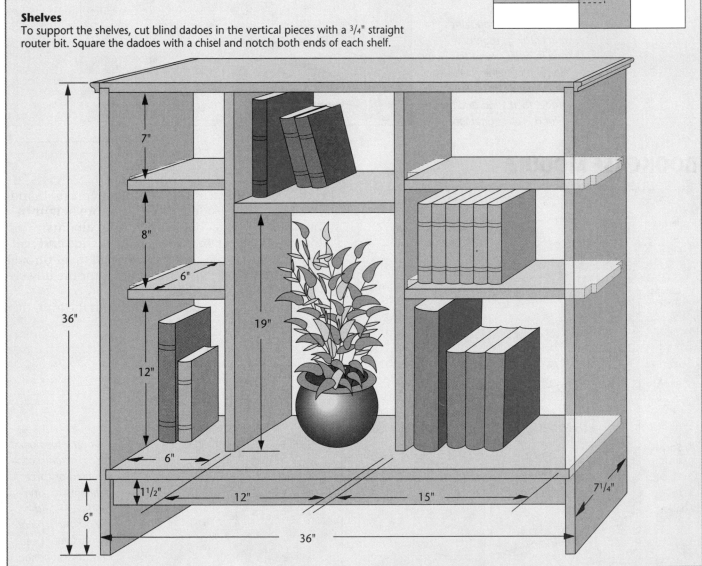

The bookcase featured above can be placed in the middle of a room or against a wall. In either case, it is sturdy enough to hold heavy books, plants, and assorted knickknacks.
DESIGN: ADAM VAN SERTIMA

WALL-TO-WALL BOOKCASE

This simple wall-to-wall bookcase is made primarily of 1x12 stock. Cut the sides to length and rout three 3/8-inch dadoes in each; space them according to the measurements given. Then, cut dadoes in the bottom and shelves for vertical shelf supports. Working with a helper, seat the bottom and sides in the dadoes; insert the shelf supports, then glue and clamp. Nail a 1x6 top to the unit, adding a single vertical support near the middle of the span. A 1x4 kickplate finishes the bottom. Sand the piece before painting or staining; or, brush on a clear finish.

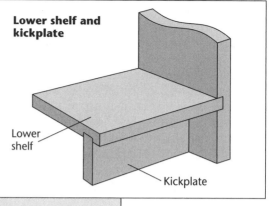

Lower shelf and kickplate

Lower shelf

Kickplate

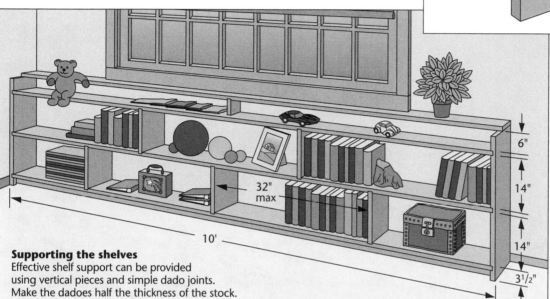

Supporting the shelves
Effective shelf support can be provided using vertical pieces and simple dado joints. Make the dadoes half the thickness of the stock.

32" max

10'

6"

14"

14"

3¹⁄₂"

Ideal for a child's room, this low-standing bookcase spans the whole length of an average-size wall. It's ideal for textbooks, toys, and writing and art materials. It's especially attractive when placed under a window, as shown.
DESIGN: COURTESY WESTERN WOOD PRODUCTS ASSOCIATION

BOOKCASE MODULE

This sturdy student bookcase is made of 1x10 lumber. Cut the sides and top to length and join the sides to the top using rabbet joints reinforced with wood screws and carpenter's glue. Countersink all screws so the heads are below the wood's surface. Mark the location for the shelves on each side of the case—they're generally spaced about 10 inches apart—routing 3/8-inch dadoes at each mark. Cut the shelves to length, adding 3/4 inch for the dadoes, and install the shelves with carpenter's glue. Add a 1x4 kickplate at the bottom and cut a piece of 1/4-inch plywood for the back; the back finishes off the piece and helps to keep it square. Conceal screw holes with wood filler, then sand the unit before painting or staining.

Although this bookcase can be built in a few hours, its simple, sturdy construction ensures that it will provide years of service. Place it near a child's desk.
DESIGN: COURTESY WESTERN WOOD PRODUCTS ASSOCIATION

FREESTANDING BOOKCASE/DIVIDER

This dual-purpose unit is made entirely of softwood lumber ranging in dimension from 1x4 to 1x12. It is assembled using simple butt joints, and the only ripping that's required is for the uprights that divide the shelving areas.

Assemble the base frame by gluing and screwing 2x4s together. Screw the uprights to the base *(see step 1 opposite)* then add a 1x4 base trim around the bottom, mitering the corners. Cut the shelves and shelf supports from 1x12 stock and attach them to the uprights as shown in step 2. Add the 1x4 top trim, mitered and glued at the corners, by nailing it to uprights *(see step 3)*. Use wood screws and glue to secure the 1x12 top and sides to the unit; attach 1x6 vertical trim in the same way. Countersink all screw heads so they are below the wood's surface. Finally, use nails and glue to attach 1½-inch half-round molding to ends of the top and ¾-inch half-round to the edges of the shelves. Conceal nail holes with wood filler; fill screw holes with wood plugs. Sand the unit and apply a protective finish.

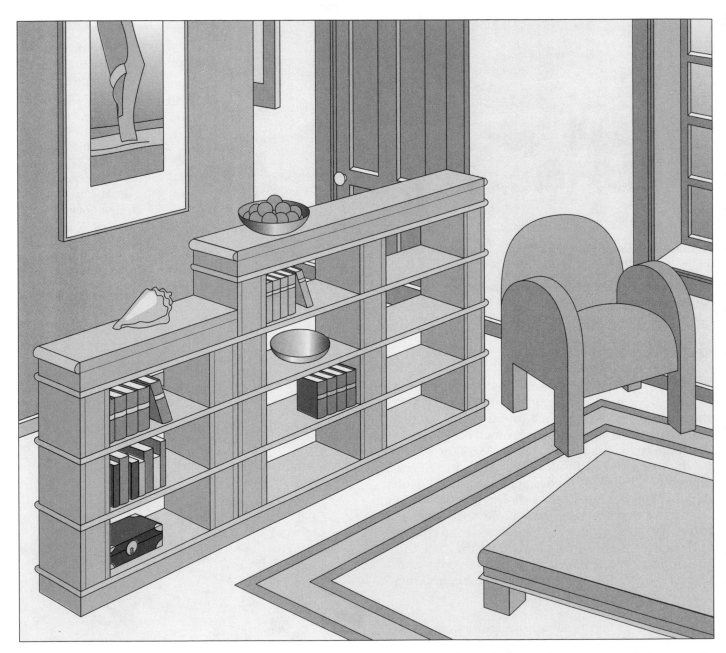

In the illustration above, the lower shelving unit was integrated with the taller one by using longer base trim and half-round edging to connect the two. Both are constructed following the basic steps shown opposite.
DESIGN: COURTESY WESTERN WOOD PRODUCTS ASSOCIATION

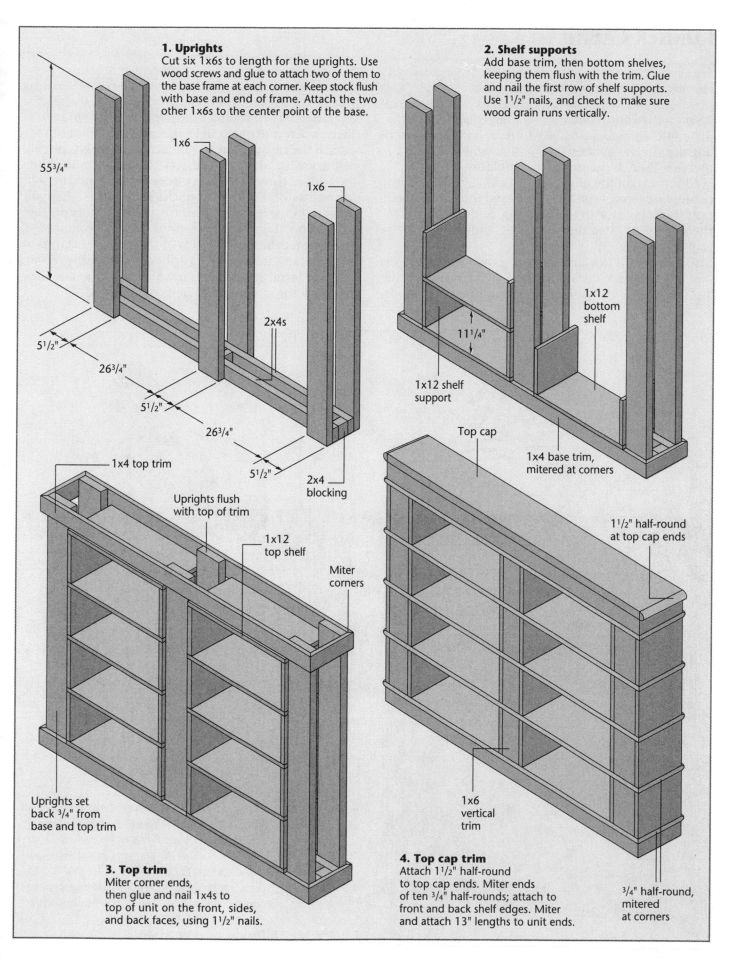

1. Uprights
Cut six 1x6s to length for the uprights. Use wood screws and glue to attach two of them to the base frame at each corner. Keep stock flush with base and end of frame. Attach the two other 1x6s to the center point of the base.

1x6

1x6

55³/₄"

5¹/₂"

26³/₄"

5¹/₂"

26³/₄"

5¹/₂"

2x4s

2x4 blocking

2. Shelf supports
Add base trim, then bottom shelves, keeping them flush with the trim. Glue and nail the first row of shelf supports. Use 1¹/₂" nails, and check to make sure wood grain runs vertically.

1x12 bottom shelf

11¹/₄"

1x12 shelf support

1x4 base trim, mitered at corners

3. Top trim
Miter corner ends, then glue and nail 1x4s to top of unit on the front, sides, and back faces, using 1¹/₂" nails.

1x4 top trim

Uprights flush with top of trim

1x12 top shelf

Miter corners

Uprights set back ³/₄" from base and top trim

4. Top cap trim
Attach 1¹/₂" half-round to top cap ends. Miter ends of ten ³/₄" half-rounds; attach to front and back shelf edges. Miter and attach 13" lengths to unit ends.

Top cap

1¹/₂" half-round at top cap ends

1x6 vertical trim

³/₄" half-round, mitered at corners

CORNER CABINET

This corner cabinet combines the timeless appeal of a classic piece of furniture with an ease of assembly made possible by modern building materials. Cut the 30- by 71-inch plywood sides; rip one long edge of each at a 45° angle—make the inside width 29¼ inches. Cut triangular shelves as shown (opposite), and a 71-inch piece of ¾-inch quarter-round molding.

Glue and nail the molding to the long, square-cut edge of one side piece. With a helper, stand this piece upright, butt the other side to the molding, and glue and nail them together. Measure, mark, cut, and nail the shelves in place through the sides.

Assemble the 1x4 faceframe as shown (opposite); glue and nail 1¼-inch decorative trim to the center of the 1x4s. Shape ¾- by ⅜-inch rabbets in the top back edge of each piece of 1¼-inch shelf trim. Cut the plywood doors ⅛ inch smaller than the frame opening.

Mount narrow strips of scrap wood along the shelf's top (below, top) and under the larger middle and bottom shelves. Screw through the strips to draw the faceframe against the carcase; angle other screws through the carcase's outside edge into the back of the faceframe. Miter the ends of three shelf trim pieces to fit against the sides of the carcase. Glue them to the shelf fronts, then add hinged doors. Install ¼-inch plate glass doors on the top section, if desired; doors need ⅛-inch clearance from the faceframe. Two sets of pivot hinges clamp to the glass and turn in holes drilled in the frame (below, bottom). Metal strike plates near the upper inside corners lock the doors against a magnetic latch.

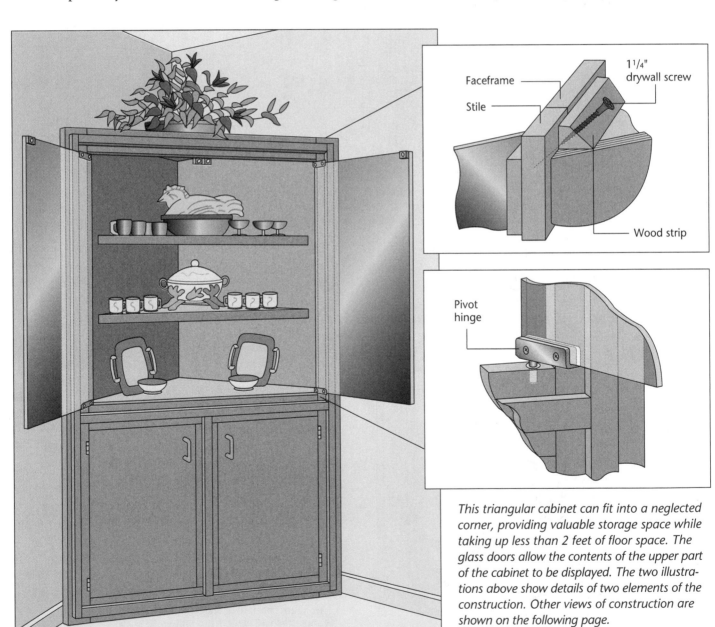

This triangular cabinet can fit into a neglected corner, providing valuable storage space while taking up less than 2 feet of floor space. The glass doors allow the contents of the upper part of the cabinet to be displayed. The two illustrations above show details of two elements of the construction. Other views of construction are shown on the following page.
DESIGN: PETER WHITELEY

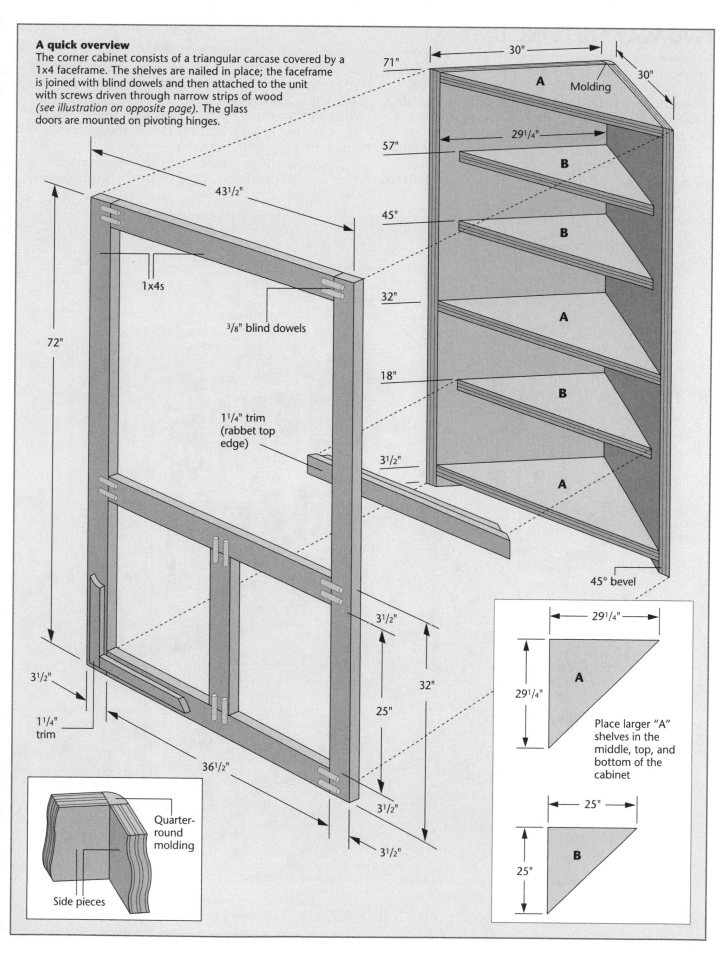

A quick overview
The corner cabinet consists of a triangular carcase covered by a 1x4 faceframe. The shelves are nailed in place; the faceframe is joined with blind dowels and then attached to the unit with screws driven through narrow strips of wood *(see illustration on opposite page)*. The glass doors are mounted on pivoting hinges.

30"

71"

30"

A   Molding

29¼"

57"   B

45"   B

1x4s

³⁄₈" blind dowels   32"   A

18"   B

72"

1¼" trim (rabbet top edge)   3½"   A

3½"   A

45° bevel

3½"

32"

3½"

25"

29¼"

A   29¼"

Place larger "A" shelves in the middle, top, and bottom of the cabinet

25"

B   25"

1¼" trim

36½"   3½"

Quarter-round molding

Side pieces

TWO-WAY SHELVING UNIT

The carcase of this handsome shelving unit is made from ³/₄-inch plywood with 1x2 lumber used for the faceframe and 1x12 for the shelving. Tack 1x2 trim to the front edges of the shelves for added decorative appeal and strength.

Cut the top, bottom, and sides to length and then rip them to 12³/₄ inches wide. Rout rabbets along the bottom and top inside edges of the sides. Rout two dadoes in the top and bottom pieces for the vertical shelf supports. Cut the supports to length, adding ³/₈ inch at the top and bottom for the dadoes, and then rip them to 12³/₄ inches wide. Rout dadoes for the shelf tracks on the inside face of the two sides, and both faces of the vertical supports.

Assemble the carcase by fitting the top and bottom into the rabbets routed in the two side pieces.

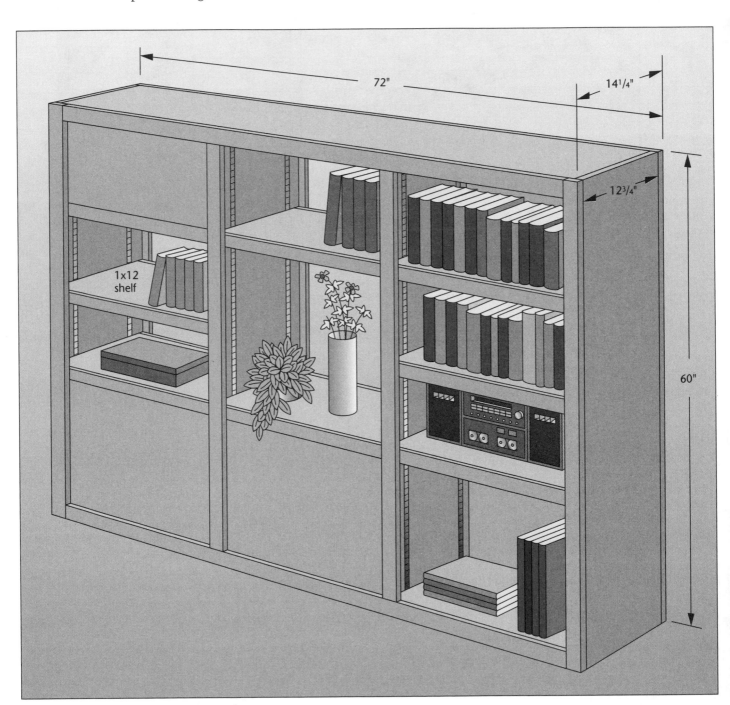

This two-way shelving unit can be accessed from either side. Not only is it an efficient way to store books and other knickknacks, it makes an attractive room divider.

Reinforce the corners with glue and fasten with finishing nails; then install the vertical supports, first adding carpenter's glue to the dadoes, and then nailing. Cut the shelves from 1x12 lumber and add wood trim to their edges. Insert the commercial shelving tracks into the grooves cut in sides and vertical supports; add clips at the appropriate height. For more information on shelf supports, turn to page 29.

Cut the plywood facings to add where desired; the facings should fit flush with the edges of the frame. Glue the facings and nail into them through the vertical supports. Add the 1x2 faceframe trim to both sides of the unit, nailing and gluing it in place.

Conceal nail holes with filler, sand, and finish with enamel or stain. If you adapt this plan to build a unit more than 5 feet tall, anchor the piece to a wall.

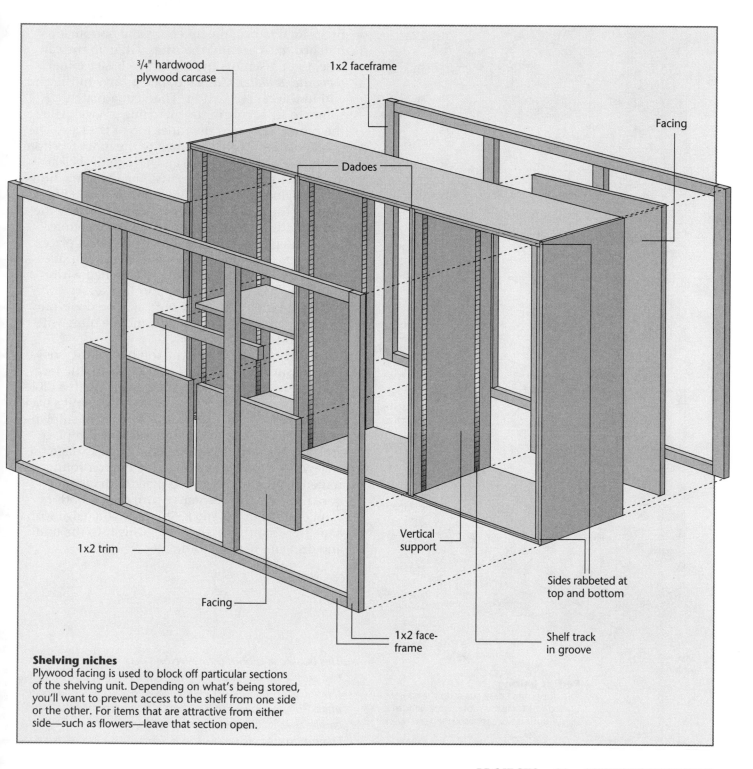

¾" hardwood plywood carcase

1x2 faceframe

Dadoes

Facing

1x2 trim

Facing

Vertical support

Sides rabbeted at top and bottom

1x2 faceframe

Shelf track in groove

Shelving niches
Plywood facing is used to block off particular sections of the shelving unit. Depending on what's being stored, you'll want to prevent access to the shelf from one side or the other. For items that are attractive from either side—such as flowers—leave that section open.

EARLY AMERICAN STYLE BOOKCASE

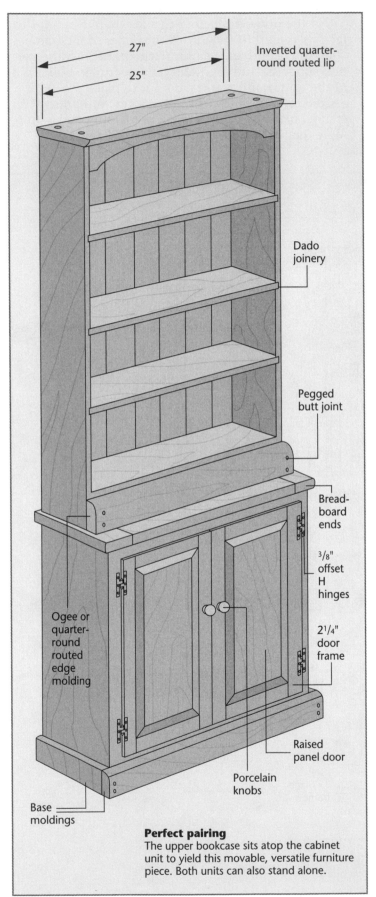

27"

25"

Inverted quarter-round routed lip

Dado joinery

Pegged butt joint

Breadboard ends

³/₈" offset H hinges

2¹/₄" door frame

Raised panel door

Porcelain knobs

Ogee or quarter-round routed edge molding

Base moldings

Perfect pairing
The upper bookcase sits atop the cabinet unit to yield this movable, versatile furniture piece. Both units can also stand alone.

Although this bookcase appears quite elaborate, it is relatively straightforward to build, using simple joinery techniques such as rabbets and dadoes. If economy is important, you can build the bookcase from No. 2 pine or even a less expensive grade and finish the wood with a stain. The bookcase is designed to make efficient use of standard-dimension lumber.

The bottom unit is assembled with dadoes and rabbets *(opposite, top)*. The front stiles have a ³/₄- by ¹/₄-inch rabbet; the inner top and bottom are notched to fit around the stiles. Glue up the carcase, then assemble the top of the base cabinet *(opposite, middle)*. Cut a stopped groove in the ends and in the center section. Then cut a matching spline to fit snugly in the matching grooves. Glue the center section to the inner top of the case. The breadboard ends are anchored to the inner top from the inside with screws driven through oval clearance holes to allow for expansion and contraction. (Do not glue the ends to the center section.) Round over the top edge of the base moldings. Attach the front molding to the carcase with screws, counterbored and plugged; secure the side pieces in place with screws (no glue) from the inside of the side panels. The back, made from 1x4s joined with shiplap joints, requires a support bracket *(opposite, bottom)* on each side at the bottom. The doors are a raised-panel design *(page 74)*, and are hung with ³/₈-inch offset hinges.

The measurements for the top part of the bookcase are shown on the facing page. Mark the location for the shelves and cut the dadoes with a table saw, radial-arm saw, or a router. The top unit's back panel is made from resawn 1x4 stock with shiplap joints. Glue up the unit with the shelves in place and attach the back with finishing nails. Shape the edges of the top with an inverted quarter-round routed lip. Secure the top in place with counterbored screws. The decorative trim on the bottom can be cut from 5/4 stock. Shape the top edge with a quarter-round or an ogee bit. Glue it to the unit and drill and peg the joint.

This bookcase is both attractive and versatile. It consists of two parts—an upper and a lower cabinet. Each part is built separately and both are designed to work also as stand-alone units. The base makes a good small cabinet, while the top can be used as a freestanding bookcase.
DESIGN: JON ARNO

ANATOMY OF TOP CABINET

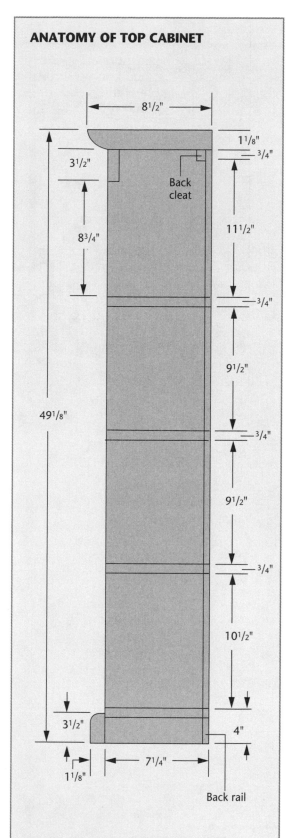

Side view with shelf locations
The anatomy above shows the placement of the shelves in the upper unit of the bookcase. These can be varied, depending on your collection, but don't place shelves much closer than 9 inches apart.

BOTTOM CABINET

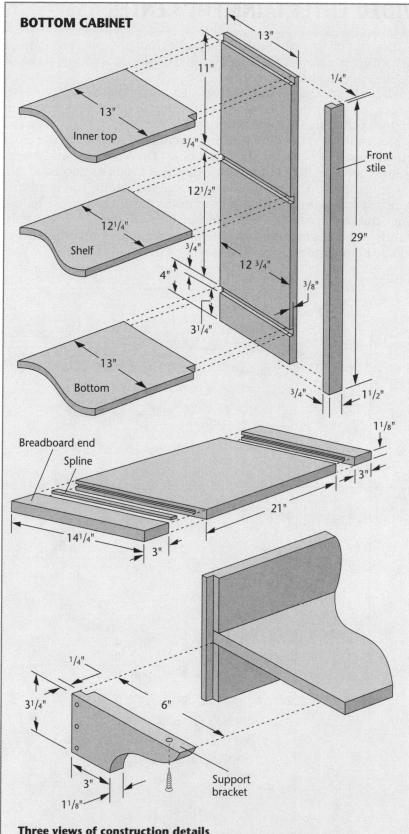

Three views of construction details
The lower cabinet consists of sides, a top, a bottom, and a shelf joined with dadoes and rabbets (above, top). The top (above, middle) features breadboard ends and a spline that meshes with a stopped groove. The case is reinforced by attaching two support brackets at each corner at the bottom of the back of the carcase (above, bottom).

VIDEO ENTERTAINMENT CENTER

Although you can build this handy unit from plywood, ⅝-inch melamine is a convenient, inexpensive choice. Make sure you band all visible edges before you assemble the piece.

All horizontal panels and shelves are attached to the side pieces using biscuit joints *(page 64)*. Vertical shelf dividers fit into dadoes routed into the bottom panel and the lower two shelves.

Mark shelf and divider locations carefully, then cut the slots for the biscuits. In this plan, the shelf that holds the television sits 21⅜ inches below the VCR shelf, but you can vary this height as needed.

For the glue-up, make sure you have all the clamps you need close at hand. Spread glue in the slots, then insert the biscuits. Work quickly—once the biscuits are inserted they will begin to swell. An extra pair of hands will make the job easier. Remember to check that the carcase is square before the glue cures.

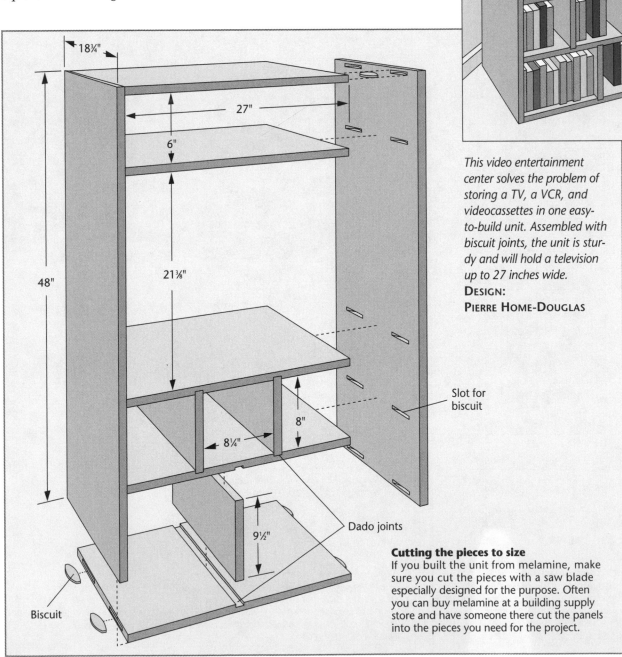

This video entertainment center solves the problem of storing a TV, a VCR, and videocassettes in one easy-to-build unit. Assembled with biscuit joints, the unit is sturdy and will hold a television up to 27 inches wide.
DESIGN:
PIERRE HOME-DOUGLAS

Cutting the pieces to size

If you built the unit from melamine, make sure you cut the pieces with a saw blade especially designed for the purpose. Often you can buy melamine at a building supply store and have someone there cut the panels into the pieces you need for the project.

ROLLING VCR CART

Like the video entertainment center on the preceding page, this rolling VCR cart is constructed from ⅝-inch melamine. The carcase is joined with rabbets cut in the side panels. The two shelves fit into dadoes—also cut in the side panels. For the back panel, use a piece of ¼-inch hardboard. Secure it in place with brads. You will need to drill holes in the back to feed wires from the TV to the VCR. Attach the overlay doors with European hinges—the same type used for kitchen cabinet doors. To complete the unit, attach simple door handles *(page 30)*, then screw casters to the underside of the base panel.

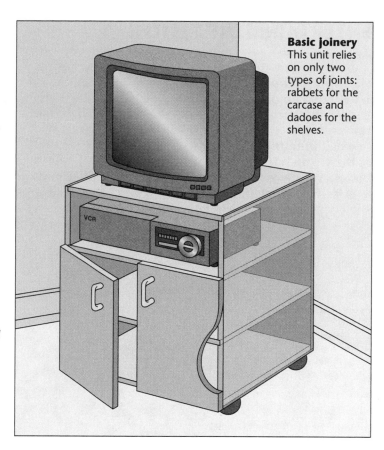

Basic joinery
This unit relies on only two types of joints: rabbets for the carcase and dadoes for the shelves.

This easy-to-build entertainment cart fits nicely in the corner of a room—and with rollers attached to the bottom, it can be moved to accommodate more guests or different viewing angles.
DESIGN: MARIO GROSLEAU

CD STORAGE SYSTEM

This CD storage system consists of shelves that rest on commercial shelf tracks and movable dividers. Begin by rounding over the front edges of a 1x8 long enough for all the shelves. Measure in 6⅜ inches from the point where the rounding stops; rip the board to this width, then cut it into 22-inch-long pieces. Cut a shallow groove for the bracket tips in the front of each shelf.

Round over the edges of a 1x2 and cut it to lengths of 22 inches. Screw them to the back of the shelves, then cut and assemble the shelf ends *(far right, top)*.

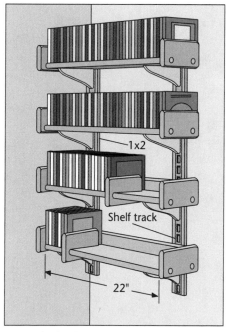

Movable dividers add versatility to this CD storage system.
DESIGN: BILL RICHTER

Cut the movable dividers from 1x8 stock; round over the edges. Mount weather stripping to the bottom piece *(right, bottom)*.

Fit shelf tracks inside grooves in the 1x2 strips. Stain the wood, then finish with varnish or lacquer. Screw the tracks and mounting strips to studs.

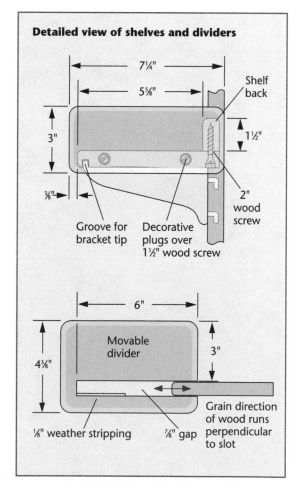

Detailed view of shelves and dividers

7¼"
5⅝"
3"
⅜"
Shelf back
1½"
2" wood screw
Groove for bracket tip
Decorative plugs over 1½" wood screw

6"
Movable divider
4⅝"
3"
⅛" weather stripping
⅞" gap
Grain direction of wood runs perpendicular to slot

ENTERTAINMENT CENTER

This simple entertainment center has room for storing electronic components on the shelves, and videocassettes and compact discs in the space behind the doors. Use 5/8-inch melamine—one 4x8 sheet will do—to build this unit. First, cut the sheet in two 4x4 pieces and rip one half into three equal panels of 16 inches. Select two of these panels for the sides, cutting rabbets along the bottom inside edge of each. Use an electric drill to drill a series of equidistant holes into each side for adjustable shelf pegs *(page 78)*. Also, rout a 3/8-inch-deep dado in

each side to fit a fixed shelf. Next, cut the third panel into two for the top and bottom; cut rabbets along the bottom edge of the top piece.

Rip the second half of the sheet into three equal panels of 16 inches. Cut one panel in half for the adjustable shelves. Cut the fixed shelf from the second panel, making it slightly longer (about 3/4 inch) than the adjustable shelves so it fits the dadoes in the side panel.

Cut the two doors from the third panel, making them each 11 1/4 inches wide. Conceal the edges (except those that will be in the back of the unit, and the ends of the fixed shelf) by attaching laminate edge-banding. Use the pieces remaining from the second and third panels to make a base for the unit. Miter the corners of the base and install triangular blocks to keep each corner at 90°.

Assemble the unit by using bolt-and-cam knockdown fittings *(page 25)* to support the joints where the sides meet the top and bottom; add glue in the dadoes for the fixed shelf. Attach the base to the cabinet from underneath, screwing through the triangular blocks. Mount the doors using European hinges *(page 27)*, making them flush with the front of the unit; see page 28 for information on catches. Use dowels for the shelf supports and cut a piece of 1/4-inch plywood for the partial back.

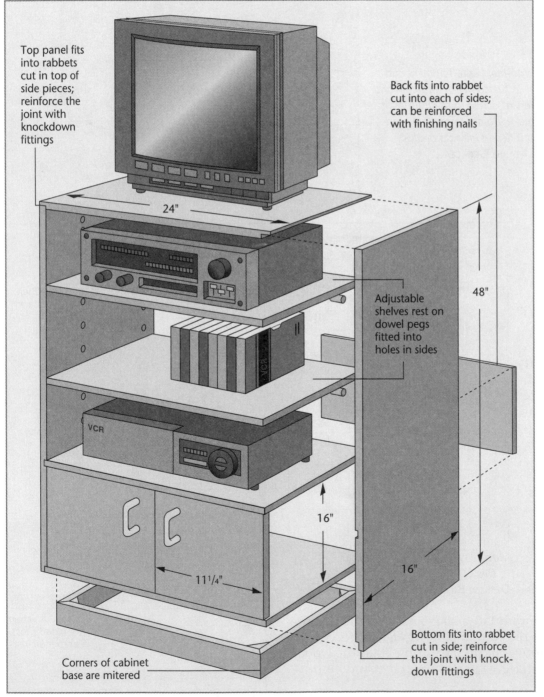

Top panel fits into rabbets cut in top of side pieces; reinforce the joint with knockdown fittings

Back fits into rabbet cut into each of sides; can be reinforced with finishing nails

24"

Adjustable shelves rest on dowel pegs fitted into holes in sides

48"

16"

VCR

16"

11 1/4"

16"

Bottom fits into rabbet cut in side; reinforce the joint with knockdown fittings

Corners of cabinet base are mitered

Although the placement of the fixed shelf is meant to provide a 16-inch space, the others can be adjusted according to the size of one's components.

DESIGN: MARIO GROSLEAU

STURDY SHELF WITH HIDDEN MOUNTING

The clean lines of this bookshelf system comes from its out-of-view mounting scheme. Cut the shelf from 2x10 stock, making it long enough to span two wall studs. Miter the ends and add dowels.

Rout a ¼-inch-deep recess near the top of each side and insert a keyhole plate *(inset)*. Attach screws to the studs at the appropriate height; sand and paint the shelf. Fit the screw heads into the keyhole slots and lower each shelf in place.

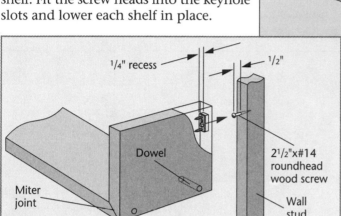

This bookshelf, which features built-in bookends, is simple in design and can be built in a couple of hours.
DESIGN: T. SCOTT MACGILLIVRAY

OPEN SHELF WITH BRACKETS

This design can accommodate nearly any open wall space. Cut the shelf to length from 2x10 stock and use scrap pieces for the brackets. Sketch the bracket design on paper first, as shown *(right, bottom)*. Transfer the design to the wood and cut out the first bracket; cut out the second bracket by using the first as a template. Cut a notch in each bracket *(right, top)* for the 1x3 ledger; shape the bracket fronts as desired.

Assemble the shelf and then mount it to the wall by screwing through the ledger strip into the studs. Recess the screws and conceal their heads with wooden buttons; this allows for easy relocation of the shelf.

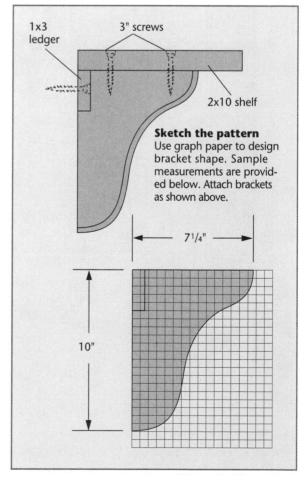

Sketch the pattern
Use graph paper to design bracket shape. Sample measurements are provided below. Attach brackets as shown above.

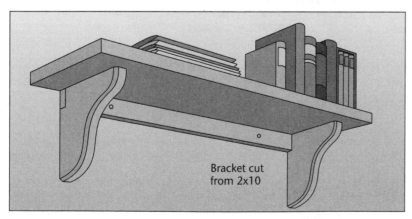

The shelf is ideal when extra book storage is needed, or for supporting plants and other decorative features that are added to a room.

CHILD'S MODULAR STORAGE SYSTEM

This multisectional unit is built from softwood lumber ranging in size from 1x3 to 1x12. The modules are sturdy and solid enough to hold a child's belongings, but not so heavy that they can't be rearranged or otherwise moved as the need arises. Because the units, such as the triangular top piece, are not secured in place, this storage system isn't suitable for very young children, who might be tempted to climb on it.

Each module is 21½ inches wide and 14½ inches deep; they vary in height from 2½ inches to 26½ inches. All corners are mitered and held fast with glue and nails; the backs are made from edge-glued 1x4s and fit into rabbets cut along the back edges of the modules.

To install the dividers in the upper module, rout dado joints in the top, bottom, and sides of the unit. Dadoes are also used to support the shelves where they meet the vertical divider. Mount all doors with invisible hinges *(page 27)*. Countersink all nail heads and conceal holes with wood filler. Sand the unit before finishing it. For a splash of color, finish the larger modules in natural wood tones, then paint the bands and base units, as well as the stools, in bright colors.

As a child grows and amasses a larger collection of toys, games, and books, add units easily to this modular storage system—merely build more boxes and stack them higher and wider.
DESIGN: COURTESY WESTERN WOOD PRODUCTS ASSOCIATION

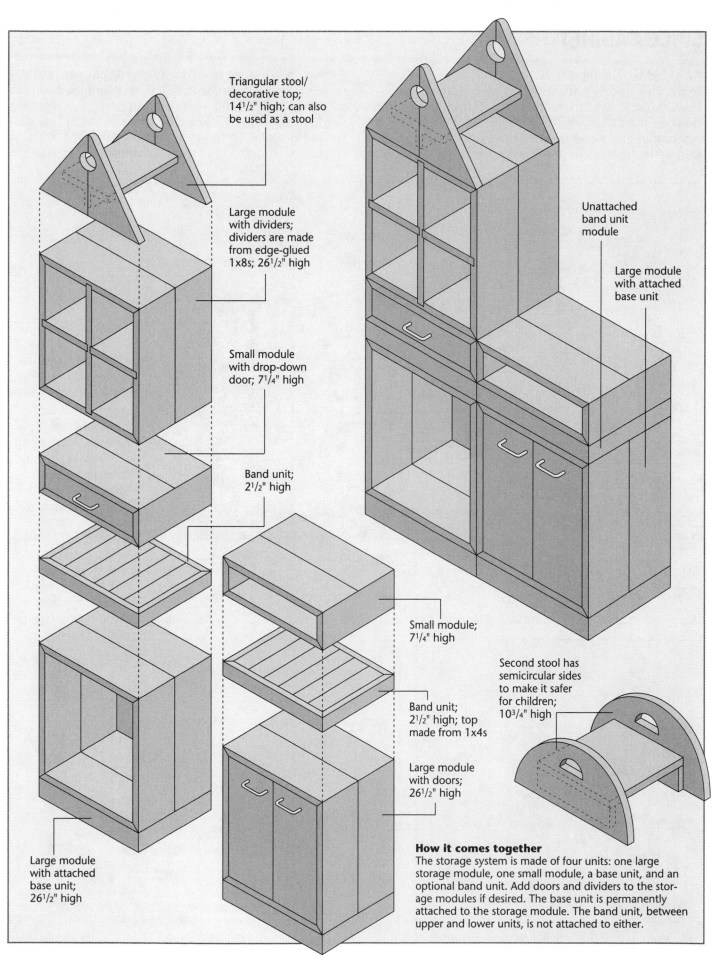

Triangular stool/ decorative top; 14$\frac{1}{2}$" high; can also be used as a stool

Large module with dividers; dividers are made from edge-glued 1x8s; 26$\frac{1}{2}$" high

Small module with drop-down door; 7$\frac{1}{4}$" high

Band unit; 2$\frac{1}{2}$" high

Large module with attached base unit; 26$\frac{1}{2}$" high

Unattached band unit module

Large module with attached base unit

Small module; 7$\frac{1}{4}$" high

Band unit; 2$\frac{1}{2}$" high; top made from 1x4s

Large module with doors; 26$\frac{1}{2}$" high

Second stool has semicircular sides to make it safer for children; 10$\frac{3}{4}$" high

How it comes together

The storage system is made of four units: one large storage module, one small module, a base unit, and an optional band unit. Add doors and dividers to the storage modules if desired. The base unit is permanently attached to the storage module. The band unit, between upper and lower units, is not attached to either.

SPICE CABINET

Any chef would appreciate this handy unit to store herbs and spices. With its doors closed, the cabinet is just 20 inches wide; when the two 3-inch doors open on their piano hinges, its width doubles. Build the cabinet frames and doors from 3/4-inch stock. Use standard joinery techniques to join the corners; a rabbet joint is a good choice (page 52). Dadoes can be cut with either a table saw and a dado head or a router equipped with a straight bit. The adjustable shelves and front lips are made from 1/4-inch stock; add an extra set of lips near the bottom of each frame. Finish the cabinet with penetrating oil; anchor it to the wall with toggle bolts.

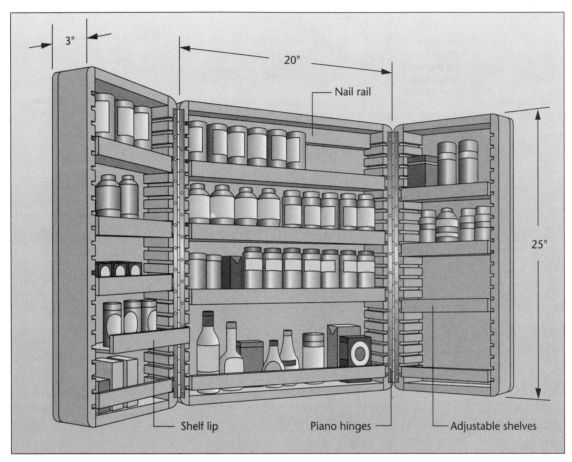

3"

20"

Nail rail

25"

Shelf lip   Piano hinges   Adjustable shelves

Shelf lips prevent the door-stored items from moving or falling. The shelves fit into dadoes cut into the sides of the cabinet. Brass-plated piano hinges provide an extra measure of strength for the spice-laden doors. Note: For adequate clearance when opening and closing the doors, plan for a space of 1/4 to 5/16 inch between them in the closed position.
DESIGN: DON GERBER

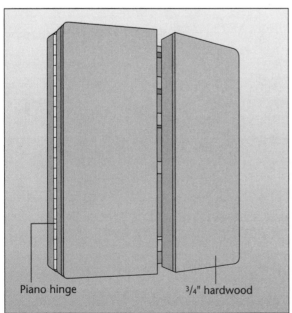

Piano hinge   3/4" hardwood

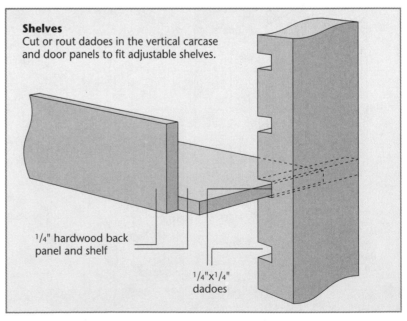

Shelves
Cut or rout dadoes in the vertical carcase and door panels to fit adjustable shelves.

1/4" hardwood back panel and shelf

1/4"x1/4" dadoes

BASIC BOOKCASE

Cut the pieces to size; use $3/4$-inch plywood for the carcase and shelves and 1x2 for the faceframe. Edge-band the front edge of the adjustable shelves, then bore the holes for the shelf pins. Glue and clamp the carcase. Once the adhesive has cured, add the back, cut from a sheet of $1/4$-inch plywood. Secure the back in place with brads, making sure the carcase is square. Join the parts of the faceframe with blind mortise-and-tenons *(page 57)*; remember to allow for the extra length of the tenons when you cut your rails for the faceframe. Glue and nail the faceframe to the carcase. The decorative molding can be fashioned from a piece of 2x2, then secured to the carcase with finishing nails. Countersink all the nails, fill in the holes with wood filler, then sand the unit before applying the finish.

The basic carcase of this bookcase is covered with a faceframe to conceal joints and end grain. Base molding and feet give the unit a more formal look, complemented by the crown molding.

DESIGN: GILES MILLER-MEAD

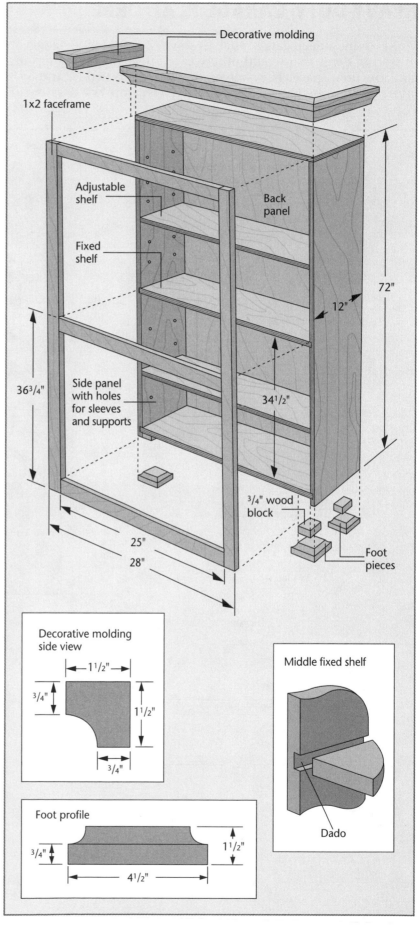

Decorative molding

1x2 faceframe

Adjustable shelf

Fixed shelf

Back panel

72"

12"

Side panel with holes for sleeves and supports

$36^3/4$"

$34^1/2$"

$3/4$" wood block

Foot pieces

25"

28"

Decorative molding side view

$1^1/2$"

$3/4$"

$1^1/2$"

$3/4$"

Middle fixed shelf

Dado

Foot profile

$3/4$"

$1^1/2$"

$4^1/2$"

HEAVY-DUTY GARAGE PLATFORM

These 30-inch-deep garage shelves solve the problem of storing items that would otherwise clutter up valuable floor space. The shelves are made from two layers of plywood glued together. They rest atop 1x4 ledger strips screwed to wall studs; their fronts are supported by threaded rods secured with couplings and eye bolts tied to screw hooks in ceiling joists or rafters. Edges are sanded smooth.

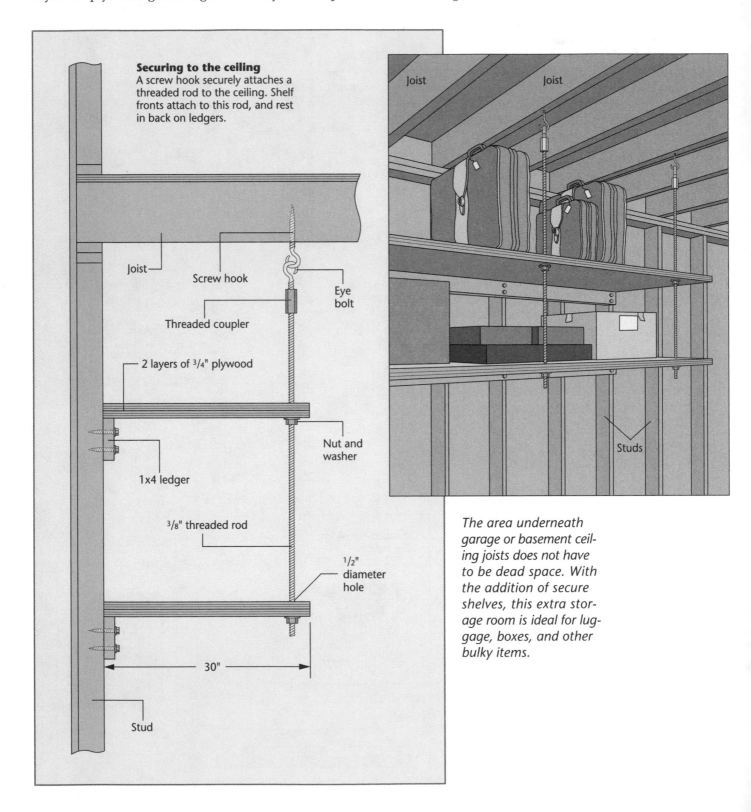

Securing to the ceiling
A screw hook securely attaches a threaded rod to the ceiling. Shelf fronts attach to this rod, and rest in back on ledgers.

Joist

Screw hook

Eye bolt

Threaded coupler

2 layers of ³/₄" plywood

Nut and washer

1x4 ledger

³/₈" threaded rod

¹/₂" diameter hole

30"

Stud

Joist

Joist

Studs

The area underneath garage or basement ceiling joists does not have to be dead space. With the addition of secure shelves, this extra storage room is ideal for luggage, boxes, and other bulky items.

BOOKSHELVES AND CABINETS GLOSSARY

Banding
A decorative edge or trim applied to a surface to hide end grain or the edges of sheet materials, such as plywood layers.

Bevel
An incline between two faces or edges, on a piece of wood. Also used to describe the incline on a tool blade. Includes any angle other than 90°.

Biscuit joint
A method of joining wood in which thin biscuitlike wafers of compressed wood fit into slots cut in mating workpieces.

Blind cut
A cut that is not visible on the outside of a joint or workpiece.

Brad
A small, almost headless nail that resembles a miniature finishing nail; useful for joining thin pieces and nailing into delicate ends or edges.

Carcase
The outer framework of a piece of furniture; boxlike construction.

Casework
Furniture construction based on the joining of panels to each other.

Counterbore
Drilling a hole in advance of setting in a screw at a depth that leaves the head of the screw below the surface of the stock. Allows for the hole to be plugged, concealing screw head.

Countersink
Beveling the opening of a hole for a flathead screw to allow the head to sit flush with the surface.

Crosscut
A cut running perpendicular to the direction of the wood grain.

Dado
A channel cut across the grain of a workpiece with square sides and flat bottom.

Ease
To remove a sharp corner with sandpaper or a plane.

Edge (of a board)
The narrow side that runs parallel to the grain direction, as compared to the end.

End (of a board)
The surface that reveals the crosscut end grain, as compared to the edge.

Extension
An addition to a guiding accessory on a machine table that facilitates the movement of stock through the cutter.

Face (of a board)
The wider surface; the good face, which will show on the finished project, is chosen for its attractive appearance.

Faceframe
A structure composed of horizontal and vertical members that gives the front of a cabinet carcase structural integrity.

Featherboard
An antikickback device designed to hold and guide a workpiece while it is being worked on a stationary power tool.

Fence
Device attached to a stationary power tool surface to guide stock. Also, the part of a tool that guides it along the edge of the stock.

Figure
The pattern formed by wood grain.

Frame-and-panel
A type of structure in which a floating (unattached) panel is supported by a grooved frame made up of rails and stiles. Commonly used to make doors.

Fret saw
A type of coping saw with the same thin, fine-toothed blade but a frame that features a much deeper throat.

Grain
The direction and arrangement of the wood fibers.

Groove
A channel cut in the edge or face of a workpiece, going with the grain.

Infeed
The end on a machine table from which a workpiece proceeds into the cutter.

Jig
Any device designed to aid the guiding of a tool or stock in motion; shop-built or commercially available.

Jointing
The process of truing stock by making an edge or a face perfectly flat, straight, and square to an adjoining surface.

Kerf
The area of a workpiece that is removed by the teeth of a saw blade.

Miter
An angled cut; a joint between two workpieces at any angle other than 90°.

Moldings
Decorative strips of wood that can be shaped with a router or a table saw.

Mortise
A shaped cutout in a workpiece that commonly receives a tenon; also a recess for a hinge.

Nominal size
The size of a piece of lumber when it is first cut from the log, before being surfaced. Lumber is sold by these sizes.

Ogee bit
A decorative router bit that produces an S-shaped profile.

Outfeed
The end on a machine table to which a workpiece proceeds after having contacted the cutter.

Pilot
The part of a router bit that guides it along the rim of a template or piece of stock.

Pilot hole
A hole drilled into a piece of stock for a screw or nail to follow. It is slightly smaller than the shaft of the nail or the threads of the screw.

Plunge cut
A cut made directly into the surface of a workpiece without starting from an open edge.

Push stick (or block)
A tool used to feed wood through the cutting blade or bit of a tool to protect the operator's hands.

Rail
The horizontal element of a framed structure which joins two stiles.

Rip cut
A cut running parallel to the direction of the wood grain.

Sheet material
Any type of manufactured or processed stock that is bought in large panel form, such as plywood or hardboard.

Shiplap joint
An edge milling where each edge of a board is rabbeted on the opposite face so that it fits into the adjacent board.

Spline
A small piece of wood that fits into matching grooves in two workpieces.

Square
The achievement of a 90° angle at the point where two workpieces meet or at the end of a board.

Stile
The vertical element of a framed structure which joins rails.

Stock
Woodworking material including solid lumber and sheet products.

Stop block
A clamped-on block of wood that prevents the stock or cutter from passing beyond a certain point.

Stopped cut
An abrupt end to a cut before an edge of the stock is reached.

Stretcher
A horizontal member providing stability between posts as in table or chair leg construction.

Surface
To work the face of a board on a jointer or with any other cutting tool to create an even and clean profile.

Template
A device, either shop-made or commercial, that guides a cutting tool along a certain path or in a design.

Tenon
The protrusion at the end of a workpiece that fits into a mortise.

Through cut
A cut that extends from edge to edge on a piece of stock.

Toenailing
The act of driving a nail at an angle through one piece into another.

Veneer
A thin slice of wood to be glued onto another surface for decorative effect or to hide lower grades of construction material.

Warp
The distortion of wood due to uneven shrinkage when drying; can also be caused by taking on moisture.

Waste
Excess material to be removed (or already removed) from stock.

INDEX